very Vegetarian Cookbook

very Vegetarian Cookbook

Over 150 delicious, colorful, and inspirational

recipes with the minimum of fuss

EDITED BY JANE DONOVAN

CHARTWELL
BOOKS, INC.

A QUINTET BOOK

Published by Chartwell Books
A Division of Book Sales, Inc.
114, Northfield Avenue
Edison, New Jersey 08837

This edition produced for sale in the U.S.A., its
territories, and dependencies only.

ISBN 0-7858-0921-X

This book was designed and produced by
Quintet Publishing Limited
6 Blundell Street
London N7 9BH

Creative Director: Richard Dewing
Art Director: Clare Reynolds
Design: Siân Keogh
Project Editor: Doreen Palamartschuk
Editor: Jane Donovan
Illustrator: Shona Cameron

Typeset in Great Britain by
Central Southern Typesetters, Eastbourne
Manufactured in Hong Kong by
Regent Publishing Services Ltd
Printed in China by
Leefung-Asco Printers Ltd

Material in this book previously appeared in:
Indian Vegetarian by Sumana Ray; *Chinese Vegetarian* by
Deh-Ta Hsiung; *Vegetarian Pizza* by Maureen Keller;
Fabulous Fruit by Moya Clarke; *Olives* and *A Feast of
Mushrooms* by Marlena Spieler; *Southern Cooking,
Salsa Cooking,* and *Cajun Cooking* by Marjie Lambert;
Low-fat Vegetarian Cooking by Jenny Stacey;
The American Harvest Cookbook and *The Eggplant
Cookbook* by Rosemary Moon.

CONTENTS

INTRODUCTION

Today vegetarian food is no longer considered the preference of cranks—it is right where it should be: firmly established in the mainstream of everyday cooking and eating. Restaurants everywhere now offer vegetarian choices as part of their menus and many people are making a conscious decision to cut down on their intake of meat, especially red meat, and high-fat foods even if they do not completely change their eating habits. As we travel more widely and through newspaper and magazine articles, as well as television programs, we are now better acquainted with the cuisine of other countries, where vegetarian cooking often features strongly. At the same time, a whole new range of ingredients is available in our supermarkets and foodstores, and we can happily shop on a global scale in most towns and cities.

THE VEGETARIAN ISSUE

Throughout the world, the number of people who decide to follow the vegetarian way of eating is growing and in tropical climates (India, for example) where meat deteriorates extremely quickly, the native inhabitants grow their own vegetables and live off the land easily, so making themselves completely self-sufficient. More and more people find that they no longer enjoy the taste of meat or they may decide to cut down on the number of cholesterol-rich foods that they eat to reduce the risk of heart disease. On the other hand, many people are simply discovering how satisfying (and

economical) it is to produce a really delicious meal that contains absolutely no meat.

THE IMPORTANCE OF GOOD INGREDIENTS

To get the best results from any recipe, always buy the freshest ingredients and watch for seasonal produce in your stores. Local farmers often sell vegetables and fruits direct or you may even decide to grow your own. If you live in a city, you could grow your own fresh herbs or plant tomatoes on the roof terrace. Also, only buy as much as you need; don't be tempted to buy in bulk or you will find that ingredients often lose their flavor, not to mention their natural goodness.

LOW FAT OR NO FAT?

Although it is recommended that fat intakes are severely reduced, everything in moderation is your best maxim. No-one is suggesting a totally fat-free diet. We all require a certain amount of fat for our bodies to function such as producing linoleic acid for skin maintenance, growth in children, and for the supply of the necessary compounds. As we cannot produce these compounds ourselves, it is vital that we obtain them from food. Fat also enhances flavor. The following regime is recommended by the American Heart Association:

Less than ten percent of our daily calories should come from saturated fats: up to ten percent may come from polyunsaturated fats, and the remainder of our calorie intake may come from

▲ *Fiber is an essential ingredient in a vegetarian diet*

monounsaturated sources. At present, the majority of the population obtains at least 40 percent of their total calorie intake from fat, so there is plenty of room for improvement.

Eating a low-fat diet (particularly a vegetarian diet) will actually improve your life and could extend life expectancy. It has been proven that those who change to a low-fat diet reduce their risk of heart disease and they are also less susceptible to gallstones, diabetes, obesity, stomach upsets, thrombosis, eczema, asthma, arthritis, and general lethargy. A low-fat and/or vegetarian diet will not only make you feel better and have more energy, you will also look better.

VEGETARIAN OR VEGAN?

Many people refer to themselves as vegetarians if they do not eat red meat, but this is inaccurate. No vegetarians eat any animal flesh, which includes poultry and fish as well as red and white meats. Vegans, those who follow the strictest vegetarian diet, will not eat anything at all that is derived from

animals—no cheese, butter or any milk-based foods; indeed some also refuse honey, which they do not believe should be taken from the bees. A creative vegan diet is one of the great culinary challenges.

Lacto-vegetarians do not eat any foods that involve the slaughter of animals, so they will not eat eggs although they do include dairy products such as cheese and milk, whereas octo-lacto vegetarians will eat eggs.

There are growing numbers of would-be vegetarians who eat fish. This is especially true of those who lead a very active life, or who are just converting to vegetarianism. Colloquially referred to as "demi-veg," this is a compromise in terms of true vegetarianism but one which many parents are happy to accept for their growing children.

FIBER—THE KEY TO HEALTHY EATING

Fiber is the most important part of the vegetarian diet, the most effective weapon against the malaise brought on by the mediocrity of processed foods. Dietary fiber forms the cell walls of plants—the super-structure or skeleton. It is unique to plants and it is therefore easy to see that a diet rich in animal proteins and fat, but lacking in cereals and vegetables can be almost totally lacking in fiber—but why should this matter?

Fiber is essential for the efficient working of the digestive system and therefore the processing of our food. A fiberless diet is easy to eat and presents little intestinal challenge. Indeed, much of the progress in the early days of the "food industry" was aimed at making eating "easier" by refining foods. However, intestinal inactivity causes disorders and disease. In the less developed

HOW TO CHANGE YOUR FAT INTAKE

Talk is cheap. Action speaks louder than words. Now that you know the reasons why you should reduce your fat intake, here are some practical pointers:

❖ Cut away visible fats in your diet, such as those used in cooking and those eaten as snacks.

❖ Eliminate high-fat potato chips, cookies, fried foods, candies, and processed foods. Substitute fat-free/low-fat chips, pretzels, and fat-free cookies.

❖ Reduce the amount of hard cheeses you use. Most contain 30–40 percent fat in relation to weight. Try using a little strong-flavored cheese rather than a lot of mild cheese.

❖ Limit egg yolks to three a week, but continue to use egg whites as often as desired.

❖ Begin to discover the aroma and flavor of fresh herbs; these can enhance your cooking without piling on the calories.

❖ Avoid fried foods. Try broiling, sautéeing, and steaming. Alternatively, try poaching in vegetable juices with herbs and spices.

❖ Skim the fat from stews, casseroles, and soups. You'll be surprised how much fat you will save.

❖ Add more grains, pulses, and beans to your diet. They are high in protein and fiber, and low in fat. If you are following a completely vegetarian diet, grains, pulses, and beans will ensure a good balance and protein.

❖ Pasta is filling, healthy, and low in fat but watch what you use in your sauces!

❖ Switch to skim milk and you will hardly notice the difference in flavor. In recipes calling for cream, use whole milk or yogurt; for whipping cream, use chilled evaporated skim milk.

❖ Substitute curd cheeses in place of cream cheeses.

countries of the world where the staple diet is rice, lentils, and vegetables there is disease, but much of it is associated with vitamin deficiencies rather than a lack of dietary fiber.

To keep healthy it is important to cook with, and eat, as many unprocessed foods as possible, which leads inevitably to a high fiber diet. What is amazing is that, even among meat-eaters, the foods that we think of as starches or carbohydrates (fiber foods) often contribute a significant amount of protein to the diet—between 20 and 30 percent of the protein in an average diet comes from potatoes. Cut out the animal proteins, which automatically lead to a reduction in fat, increase fiber-rich foods, and a healthy diet is easily achieved.

EXTRA PROTEINS FOR VEGETARIANS

Vegetable protein foods are becoming more and more common, and there is quite a movement in agriculture towards soya, a high protein crop which can be used as solids or liquid and which produces a much better protein yield per hectare than

▲ *A balanced diet is essential for all vegetarians*

livestock. This is regarded as one of the more plausible ways of increasing the quality of the international diet.

Tofu, or bean curd, a recent introduction to many Westerners but a staple protein food of the Chinese for many thousands of years, also has a valuable place in the vegetarian diet. It is bean curd and is also known as soyabean curd. Beancurd is best used fresh when the texture is firm. Natural or smoked tofu may be sliced and quickly fried, then added to salads and other vegetable dishes, or beaten into fillings for pies and flans.

ROBUST FLAVORS FOR ROBUST FOODS

Many beans and vegetables respond deliciously to clever and inventive use of herbs and spices. Roasting your own whole spices, such as cumin and coriander seeds, in a dry pan and grinding them just before use achieves the best possible flavor. Alternatively, buy small quantities of ground spices and replace them regularly. Dried seasonings arc only at their best for a few months and certainly cease to pack a punch after a year.

Fresh herbs have the best flavor, but they can be very expensive, especially if you have to buy them from a supermarket. Keep freeze-dried herbs for emergencies but, if you are lucky enough to have a herb garden, do try to use fresh leaves whenever possible. Herbs for garnish should be chopped and added at the last moment, to retain both color and immediacy of flavor. Even if you do not have a garden it is a good idea to grow some herbs in pots on your windowsill—some varieties, such as basil, are indeed better this way than outside in an unreliable climate.

One of the most exciting trends in popular cooking in the last few years has been the use of salsas as salad garnishes, and these work especially well with bean-based dishes. A mixture as simple as orange, tomatoes, scallions, and roasted mustard seeds with fresh cilantro and a chopped chile can add the most exciting explosion of color, texture, and flavor to a casserole or bake.

▲ *Fresh herbs are a flavorful addition to many vegetarian dishes*

The recipes that we have selected for the *Very Vegetarian Cookbook* prove just how varied and interesting a vegetarian diet can be. They may even inspire you to start experimenting with your own ideas. Whether you are a vegetarian already or just want some ideas for a healthier way of eating, you will find plenty of suggestions for every kind of meal including breakfasts and brunches, light suppers and lunches, and some classic vegetarian dishes. Happy cooking and eating!

BREAKFASTS AND BRUNCHES

APRICOT YOGURT CRUNCH

Serves 4

A variation on a Scottish dish, the crunchy oatmeal, spicy yogurt, and lightly poached fruit make an attractive morning dish.

INGREDIENTS

10 oz apricots, pitted

3 Tbsp honey

²/₃ cup oatmeal, toasted

¹/₂–1 tsp ground ginger

1¹/₄ cups low-fat plain yogurt

Place the apricots in a pan with ²/₃ cup water and 1 tablespoon of the honey. Cook for 5 minutes until softened and drain. Mix the oatmeal and remaining honey in a bowl. Stir the ginger into the yogurt. Alternately layer the fruit, yogurt, and oatmeal mixtures into serving glasses. Chill and serve.

OATMEAL WITH POACHED FRUIT

Serves 4

A quick oatmeal which can be made in advance or the night before. Hearty and filling, the poached fruit sets it off perfectly.

INGREDIENTS

1²/₃ cups oatmeal

4¹/₄ cups skim milk

6 oz plums, halved, pitted, and sliced

8 Tbsp honey

Place the oatmeal in a pan with the milk. Bring to a boil, reduce the heat, and simmer for 5 minutes, stirring, until thickened.

Meanwhile, place the plums in a saucepan with 2 tablespoons of the honey and ²/₃ cup water. Bring to a boil, reduce the heat, and simmer for 5 minutes until softened. Drain well.

Spoon the oatmeal into individual bowls and top with the poached plums. Serve piping hot and pour over the remaining 6 tablespoons of honey, to taste.

◀ *Apricot Yogurt Crunch*

CRUNCHY MORNING BISCUITS

Makes 14

These lightly spiced biscuits are delicious served piping hot with cinnamon yogurt,
thus eliminating the necessity for butter.

INGREDIENTS

1 cup self-rising flour

1 cup whole wheat self-rising flour

Pinch of ground cinnamon

Pinch of ground nutmeg

2 Tbsp polyunsaturated margarine

2 oz All Bran cereal

1 Tbsp chopped, skinned filberts

3 Tbsp golden raisins

1 egg

6 Tbsp skim milk

For the cinnamon yogurt

$^2/_3$ cup low-fat plain yogurt

$^1/_4$ tsp ground cinnamon

$^1/_2$ tsp honey

Preheat a 400°F oven. Place the flours and spices in a bowl and rub in the margarine to resemble fine bread crumbs. Stir in the All Bran, filberts, and raisins. Stir in the egg and milk and bring together to form a soft dough.

Knead the dough on a lightly floured surface and cut into eight 3-inch rounds. Brush the tops with a little extra milk and place on a floured baking sheet. Bake for 20 minutes until risen and golden. Mix together the yogurt ingredients and serve with the warm biscuits.

BROILED PINK GRAPEFRUIT

Serves 4

A quick, simple breakfast; it may be speedy but its flavor is sensational.

INGREDIENTS

2 Florida pink grapefruit

2 Tbsp honey

Pinch of ground allspice

Mint sprigs, to garnish (optional)

Cut the skin away from the grapefruit, remove any remaining pith, and cut each grapefruit into quarters. Place the quarters in a heatproof shallow dish.

Mix together the honey and allspice and spoon over the grapefruit pieces. Cook under the broiler for 5 minutes. Serve garnished with mint, if desired.

BREAKFAST HASH

Makes 4

*For a speedier breakfast, cook the potatoes for this tasty dish the evening before
and store in a sealed bag in the refrigerator until required.*

INGREDIENTS

3 cups peeled, cubed potatoes

1 Tbsp sunflower oil

1 red bell pepper, halved and seeded

1 green bell pepper, halved and seeded

2 tomatoes, diced

*1½ cups open cap mushrooms, peeled,
and quartered*

2 Tbsp chopped fresh parsley

Ground black pepper

Cook the potatoes in boiling water for 7 minutes, drain well. Heat the sunflower oil in a large skillet, add the potatoes, and cook for 10 minutes, stirring.

Chop the red and green bell peppers and add to the skillet with the tomatoes and mushrooms. Cook for 5 minutes, stirring constantly. Add the chopped parsley, season to taste, and serve.

FRUIT KABOBS

Serves 4

The perfect way to present fresh fruit, these lightly broiled kabobs, with a hint of mint, make a refreshing start to the day.

INGREDIENTS

2 Tbsp fine granulated sugar

2 mint sprigs, plus extra to garnish

1 papaya, halved, seeded, and chopped into 2-inch squares

1 mango, pitted and chopped into 2-inch squares

1 star fruit, sliced

2 Chinese gooseberries, sliced thick

Soak four wooden skewers in water for 30 minutes. Remove when ready to use. Place the sugar, mint, and $^2/_3$ cup water in a pan. Heat gently to dissolve the sugar and then bring to a boil until reduced by half. Discard the mint.

Thread the fruit onto the skewers, alternating the varieties. Brush with the syrup and broil for 10 minutes, turning and brushing until heated through. Serve hot, garnished with mint.

STRAWBERRY COCKTAIL

Serves 4

A refreshing breakfast cocktail with a sparkle. It is as quick and easy to make as it is to drink.

INGREDIENTS

8 oz strawberries, hulled and chopped

$^3/_4$ cup cranberry juice

2 Tbsp honey

$^1/_2$ tsp ground ginger

2 cups sparkling mineral water

Ice and mint sprigs, to serve

4 whole strawberries, to garnish

Place the strawberries, cranberry juice, honey, and ginger in a food processor and blend for 30 seconds until smooth and creamy.

Add the sparkling mineral water, ice, and mint. Pour into glasses, garnish with the strawberries, and serve immediately.

HASH-BROWN POTATOES WITH BAKED BEANS

Serves 6

These golden potato cakes are served with a spicy bean dish, and are perfect for mopping up the delicious juices.
Make the bean dish in advance and keep in the refrigerator until morning.
Simply heat the beans in a pan over gentle heat.

INGREDIENTS

For the baked beans

1¼ cups dried navy beans, soaked
overnight

⅔ cup vegetable broth

½ tsp dried mustard

1 onion, chopped

2 Tbsp dark molasses

1 cup tomatoes, peeled, and chopped

1 Tbsp tomato paste

1 Tbsp chopped fresh basil

Ground black pepper

For the potato cakes

3 cups peeled, cubed potatoes

2 Tbsp skim milk

1 onion, chopped

1 garlic clove, minced

2 tsp sunflower oil

Drain the soaked beans and rinse well under cold water. Drain and put in a large saucepan with 2 cups of water. Bring the beans to a boil and boil rapidly for 10 minutes. Reduce the heat to a simmer, cover and cook for 1 hour or until the beans are cooked, topping up the water, if necessary. Drain the beans and return them to the pan. Stir in the vegetable broth, dried mustard, onion, molasses, tomatoes, tomato paste, and basil. Season well and cook for 15 minutes or until the vegetables have cooked.

Make the potato cakes while the beans are cooking. Cook the potatoes in boiling water for 20 minutes or until just soft. Drain well and mash with the milk.

Add the onion and garlic, mixing well, and form into 12 equal-sized cakes. Brush a nonstick skillet with the sunflower oil and warm over medium heat. Cook the potato cakes for 15 to 20 minutes, turning once, until golden brown. Serve piping hot with the baked beans.

BREAKFAST CRUNCH

Serves 4–6

A delicious breakfast in a bowl, packed with goodness.

INGREDIENTS

¼ cup sunflower seeds

¼ cup pine kernels

¼ cup sesame seeds

2 oranges

2 Tbsp brown sugar

½ cup dried figs, chopped

2 large bananas

2½ cups Greek yogurt

Using a dry skillet, roast the sunflower seeds and pine kernels for 3 minutes over medium heat, then add the sesame seeds and roast for a further 3 minutes, stirring to give even browning. Remove the pan from the heat.

Coarsely grate the peel from 1 orange and add to the pan with the sugar and dried figs. Stir until well combined and cook for 2 minutes. Leave to cool.

Remove the peel and pith from the oranges and cut them into pieces. Slice the bananas and mix with the oranges and yogurt, divide among four dishes and top each with the fig and seeds mixture. Serve at once.

BREAD PUDDING

Serves 8

Renowned as a delicious dish, this savory bread pudding is the perfect example
of adapting a recipe to low-fat without compromising on taste.

INGREDIENTS

6 slices whole wheat bread, with
crusts removed

1 Tbsp polyunsaturated margarine

1 red bell pepper, halved and seeded

1 green bell pepper, halved and seeded

2 tomatoes, chopped

½ cup low-fat Cheddar cheese, shredded

2 egg whites, beaten

2 cups skim milk

Ground black pepper

Spread the bread with the margarine and cut each slice into four triangles by cutting on the diagonal.

Place the bell peppers skin side uppermost on a rack and broil for 10 minutes until slightly blackened. Place in a polythene bag with tongs, seal, and let cool. Peel off the skins and discard. Slice the bell peppers into thin strips.

Layer the bread, peppers, tomatoes, and half of the cheese in a large, shallow ovenproof dish. Mix the egg whites and milk together and pour over the bread. Allow to sit for 30 minutes.

Sprinkle the remaining cheese over the dish and season. Cook in the oven at 325°F for 45 minutes until set and risen. Serve hot.

APPLE DROP BISCUITS

Serves 4

This healthy version of a breakfast favorite is filled with chunks of crisp apple
which are complemented by the cinnamon spiced yogurt sauce.

INGREDIENTS

For the biscuits		For the yogurt sauce
½ cup whole wheat flour	⅓ cup skim milk	⅔ cup low-fat plain yogurt
1 tsp baking powder	1 green dessert apple, cored and chopped	½ tsp ground cinnamon
1 tsp superfine sugar	1 Tbsp raisins	1 tsp honey
1 medium egg, beaten	Vegetable oil	

Sift the flour and baking powder for the biscuits into a mixing bowl and stir in the sugar. Make a well in the center and beat in the egg and milk to make a smooth batter. Stir in the apple and raisins, mixing well.

Brush a heavy pan with a little oil and warm over medium heat. Divide the batter into eight equal portions and drop four portions into the pan, spacing them well apart. Cook for 2 to 3 minutes until the top of each drop biscuit begins to bubble. Turn the biscuits over and cook for 1 minute. Transfer to a warmed plate while cooking the remaining four biscuits.

Mix the yogurt sauce ingredients together in a bowl. Serve with the hot drop biscuits.

BANANA ENERGY

Serves 4

If you can't face a full breakfast in the morning, take your energy in a glass with
this nutritious drink.

INGREDIENTS

4 large bananas, peeled and cut into chunks

1 Tbsp lemon juice

1¼ cups low-fat plain yogurt

1¼ cups skim milk

2 Tbsp honey

Lemon slices and mint sprigs, to garnish

Place all the ingredients in a food processor or blender. Blend for 1 minute until smooth and creamy. Pour into tall serving glasses, garnish with the lemon and mint, and serve immediately.

Apple Drop Biscuits ▶

SPICED PEARS

Serves 4

The aroma from this dish is almost as good as the taste, and all part of the enjoyment.
If you like, serve with a spoonful of plain yogurt or cottage cheese.

INGREDIENTS

4 large ripe pears, peeled, halved, and cored

1¼ cups mango juice

1 cinnamon stick, crushed

½ tsp grated nutmeg

3 Tbsp raisins

2 Tbsp granulated brown sugar

Place the pear halves in a pan with the fruit juice, spices, raisins, and sugar. Heat gently to dissolve the sugar and then bring to a boil.

Reduce the heat to a simmer and cook for 10 minutes more until the pears are softened. Serve hot with the syrup.

SPICY FRUIT SALAD

Serves 4

Dried fruits are filled with goodness and have a delicious, concentrated flavor of their own. With many varieties now available it is easy to mix delicious combinations to create your personal favorite fruit salad.

INGREDIENTS

½ cup dried apricots

½ cup dried peaches

½ cup dried mango

½ cup dried pears

½ cup dried pitted prunes

1 tsp ground cinnamon

3¾ cups orange juice

3 mint sprigs

⅔ cup low-fat plain yogurt

Grated rind of 1 orange

Place the fruits in a bowl and add the cinnamon and orange juice. Cover and let soak overnight.

Place the contents of the bowl in a saucepan with the mint and bring to a boil, reduce the heat to a simmer, and cook for 20 minutes until the fruits have softened. Cool and transfer to the refrigerator. Cover until required.

Remove the mint from the salad. Mix together the yogurt and orange rind. Serve with the fruit salad.

Spiced Pears ▶

APPETIZERS AND SOUPS

STAR FRUIT AND ARUGULA SALAD WITH RASPBERRY VINEGAR DRESSING

Serves 4

This makes a very good side salad or appetizer. Arugula has a strong, very distinctive flavor which is excellent when balanced with sweet salad greens such as iceberg or Romaine lettuce, but do not be tempted to add too much arugula or cut it too coarsely as it will overpower the other delicate ingredients, especially the star fruit. If arugula is not available, a bunch or two of watercress may be used instead.

INGREDIENTS

½ iceberg lettuce, shredded

12 medium arugula leaves, finely shredded

3 scallions or green onions, chopped

2 star fruit, sliced and quartered

For the dressing

3 Tbsp raspberry vinegar

1 tsp superfine sugar

Salt and ground black pepper

8 Tbsp olive oil

Toss the lettuce, arugula, and scallions together in a salad bowl. Next make the dressing: place the vinegar in a basin and whisk in the superfine sugar with plenty of seasoning. Continue whisking until the sugar and salt have dissolved. Slowly add the olive oil, whisking all the time to combine the ingredients well.

Add the star fruit to the salad. Pour the dressing over and mix lightly. Serve at once. Do not leave the star fruit to stand for any length of time once it is cut as it dries on the surface and tends to discolor slightly around the edges.

PITA OR NAAN BREAD WITH FETA-YOGURT, OLIVE OIL, AND DUKKAH

Serves 4

Bread and olive oil, with a tangy mound of feta-yogurt spread, and a sprinkling of the Middle-Eastern spice-and-nut mixture, called dukkah, is the classic breakfast throughout the Middle East. It also makes a great mid-afternoon snack or a good appetizer to prepare with any Middle-Eastern oils (if you have access to them) such as Lebanese or Israeli, though it is delicious made with any good, extra virgin olive oil.

INGREDIENTS

3 garlic cloves, chopped

4–6 oz feta cheese, crumbled

3–4 Tbsp yogurt

Extra virgin olive oil, as needed

½–1 tsp each: ground coriander, cumin, and thyme

1–2 tsp sumac

2–3 Tbsp each: coarsely ground, toasted sesame seeds, and hazelnuts or almonds

To garnish

10–15 Mediterranean black olives, or as many as you like

3–5 scallions

4–8 warm pita-bread pockets or 2–4 warm naan breads, torn into pieces and wrapped in a cloth

Combine the chopped garlic with the crumbled feta, yogurt, and 1 to 2 tablespoons of olive oil. Mound onto a plate. Combine the coriander, cumin, thyme, sumac, sesame seeds, and nuts to make *dukkah*. Pour a few tablespoons of olive oil onto a saucer and sprinkle with the *dukkah* mixture. Garnish with the olives and scallions.

Serve the plate of cheese mixture and the olive oil–spice platter with the pita or naan. Let each person dip into the various mixtures as desired, combining to taste.

ASPARAGUS WITH BELL PEPPER SAUCE

Serves 4

This bright red bell pepper sauce looks terrific spooned over asparagus spears. If you don't want to make a spicy sauce, either reduce the amount of chili sauce added, or omit it altogether.

INGREDIENTS

For the sauce	Juice of 1 lemon
3 red bell peppers, halved and seeded	1 garlic clove, minced
2 cups vegetable broth	1 lb asparagus spears, trimmed
1 tsp chili sauce	Grated rind of 1 lemon
	Parsley sprigs, to garnish

To make the sauce, cook the bell peppers under a hot broiler, skin side uppermost, for 5 minutes until the skin begins to blacken and blister. Transfer the peppers to a polythene bag using tongs, seal, and leave for 20 minutes. Peel the skin from the bell peppers and discard.

Roughly chop the bell peppers and put them in a saucepan with the broth, chili sauce, lemon juice, and garlic.

Cook over gentle heat for 20 minutes or until the bell peppers are tender. Transfer the sauce to a food processor and blend for 10 seconds. Return the purée to the saucepan and heat through gently.

Meanwhile, tie the asparagus spears into four equal bundles. Stand upright in a steamer or saucepan filled with boiling water and cook for 10 to 15 minutes until tender. Remove the asparagus from the pan and untie the bundles. Arrange on four serving plates and spoon the sauce over the top. Sprinkle the lemon rind on top, garnish with parsley, and serve.

MEDITERRANEAN TOASTS

Serves 4

These bite-sized hot open sandwiches are delicious as a snack or appetizer. Use a small crusty bread
such as Italian ciabatta or a French stick if preferred, using eight slices in place of four.
Be sure to cook these just before serving for full flavor.

INGREDIENTS

4 large, thick slices of crusty bread	1 Tbsp tomato paste
2 garlic cloves, minced	4 pitted black olives, chopped
1 Tbsp low-fat polyunsaturated spread, melted	Ground black pepper
	Basil sprigs, to garnish
4 ripe tomatoes, peeled and chopped	

Toast the slices of bread under the broiler for 2 minutes each side. Mix the garlic and melted low-fat spread together and drizzle onto one side of the toasted bread.

Mix the tomatoes, tomato paste, and olives together, season, and spoon onto the toast. Cook under the broiler for 2 to 3 minutes or until hot. Remove the toasts from under the broiler and cut in half. Garnish with basil and serve.

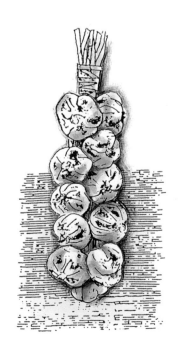

BAKED POTATO SKINS

Serves 4

Always a firm favorite, remember to prepare the skins a day in advance for ease and speed.
Pop them in the oven to warm them through before serving.

INGREDIENTS

4 medium baking potatoes

Salt as needed

For the yogurt dip

⅔ cup low-fat plain yogurt

2 garlic cloves, minced

1 Tbsp sliced scallions

For the mustard sauce

⅔ cup low-fat plain yogurt

2 tsp whole grain mustard

1 jalapeño chile, chopped

For the tomato salsa

2 medium tomatoes, chopped

3 Tbsp chopped fine red onion

1 Tbsp chopped fresh parsley

1 green bell pepper, seeded and chopped

Pinch of sugar

Scrub the potatoes and place on a baking sheet. Cook in a 400°F oven for 1 hour or until soft. Remove and cool. Cut the potatoes in half lengthwise and scoop out the centers with a teaspoon, leaving a ½-inch thickness shell. Sprinkle the skins with salt and place the potatoes in the oven for 10 minutes or until crisp.

Mix the yogurt dip ingredients together. Mix together the mustard sauce ingredients. Finally mix the tomato salsa ingredients together. Place each dip in a separate bowl and cover until required. Serve with hot potato wedges.

TOMATO-BASIL SOUP WITH RED BELL PEPPER SALSA

Serves 4

This is a delightful hot-weather soup, perfect for late summer when the garden is producing an abundance of tomatoes. Don't use hard, pink, prepacked tomatoes, since this recipe relies on the lush flavor of ripe tomatoes. The soup should be made early in the day, then chilled until serving time.

INGREDIENTS

2 garlic cloves, minced	3 Tbsp extra virgin olive oil	1 Tbsp balsamic vinegar
5 Tbsp chopped fresh basil	4 lb ripe tomatoes	½ tsp salt
¼ tsp ground black pepper	8 fl oz chicken broth	3 oz red bell pepper salsa (see page 36)

In a small bowl, mix together the garlic, 1 tablespoon basil, the black pepper, and olive oil. Lightly crush the garlic with the back of a spoon to release the juices into the oil. Let the mixture steep while you prepare the tomatoes.

Skin the tomatoes by dropping them into a pan of boiling water for about 40 seconds. Let them cool slightly, then slip off the skins. Cut them in half and squeeze out the seeds. Core and coarsely chop the tomatoes.

Put the tomatoes, chicken broth, and garlic-oil mixture into a medium-sized saucepan. Bring to a boil, then reduce the heat to low, and simmer, uncovered, for 1 hour. Add the remaining basil, the balsamic vinegar, and salt, then purée the soup. Taste and adjust the seasonings. Chill until serving time.

Top each bowl of soup with 1 to 2 tablespoons of red bell pepper salsa.

CORN CHOWDER

Serves 4

A classic chowder never loses its appeal. Prepare in advance and freeze in convenient portion sizes for ease.

INGREDIENTS

10 oz drained, canned corn kernels	³/₄ cup low-fat Cheddar or Edam cheese, shredded
2¹/₂ cups vegetable broth	1 Tbsp fresh snipped chives
1 red onion, diced	Ground black pepper
1 green bell pepper, seeded and diced	Snipped chives, to garnish
2¹/₂ cups skim milk	
2 Tbsp cornstarch	

Place the corn, broth, onion, and bell pepper in a pan. Blend 4 tablespoons of milk with the cornstarch to form a paste.

Bring the pan contents to a boil, reduce the heat, and simmer for 20 minutes. Add the milk and cornstarch paste and bring to a boil, stirring until thickened. Stir in the cheese and chives and season. Heat until the cheese has melted, garnish, and serve.

RED BELL PEPPER SALSA

Makes about 1¹/₂ cups

INGREDIENTS

4 red bell peppers

2 x ¹/₂-inch-thick slices of onion, peeled

3 garlic cloves, unpeeled

2 serrano chiles, chopped and partly seeded

2 Tbsp olive oil

1 Tbsp chopped fresh basil

1 tsp grated lemon rind

2 Tbsp red wine vinegar

¹/₄ tsp salt

To roast the bell peppers, cut them into 4 or 5 pieces lengthwise. Place the bell peppers, onion slices, and unpeeled garlic on a barbecue or under the broiler. The garlic should soften slightly, but needs to be watched closely as it scorches easily and turns bitter. The onions should be turned once, and should be softened and slightly browned. The skin of the bell peppers should be blistered and blackened, but take care not to char them so completely that the flesh is burned.

Remove the bell peppers from the fire or the broiler as they blacken. As you remove them, place them in a bag, a foil pouch, or a covered bowl.

Pull the skin off the bell peppers after 10 minutes. Because they have a tendency to get stringy lengthwise, cut them into several strips across their width. Peel the garlic cloves. Cut each onion slice into quarters. Put the bell peppers, onions, and garlic into a blender or food processor with the remaining ingredients. Process until the ingredients are well chopped but not so finely chopped that the salsa turns into a paste. Taste and adjust the seasoning.

Corn Chowder ▶

ZUCCHINI AND MINT SOUP

Serves 4

This delicate soup may be served both hot or cold. If serving hot, stir in the yogurt once the soup has been blended, garnish, and serve immediately with hot bread or croutons.

INGREDIENTS

$3^1/_2$ cups vegetable broth

1 onion, chopped

1 garlic clove, minced

3 zucchini, shredded

1 large potato, scrubbed and chopped

1 Tbsp chopped fresh mint

Ground black pepper

$^2/_3$ cup low-fat plain yogurt

Mint sprigs and zucchini strips, to garnish

Put half of the vegetable broth in a large saucepan, add the onion and garlic, and cook for 5 minutes over gentle heat until the onion softens. Add the shredded zucchini, potato, and the remaining broth. Stir in the mint and cook over gentle heat for 20 minutes or until the potato is cooked.

Let the soup cool slightly. Transfer the soup to a food processor and blend lightly for 10 seconds, until almost smooth. Turn the soup into a bowl, season, and stir in the yogurt. Cover and chill for 2 hours. Spoon the soup into individual serving bowls or a soup tureen, garnish, and serve.

NACHOS

Serves 3–4

Homemade nachos are easy to make, and with real cheese and lots of extras they're better than most commercial versions. The joy of homemade nachos is that you can prepare them to suit your own taste. This deluxe version calls for tomatoes, avocados, olives, scallions, and salsa.

INGREDIENTS

11 oz tortilla chips	1/4 cup chopped scallions
12 oz Cheddar cheese, shredded	1/2 cup black olives, pitted and sliced
2 or 3 jalapeño chiles, fresh or canned, cut crosswise into thin slices	1 large ripe avocado, peeled, stoned, and diced
2 medium tomatoes, seeded and chopped	2/3 cup tomato-based salsa

Preheat a 400°F oven. Mound the tortilla chips on one or two ovenproof serving platters, layering with the cheese and jalapeños. Bake until the cheese is melted, 3 to 5 minutes. Remove from the oven and sprinkle with the tomatoes, scallions, olives, and avocados. Serve with salsa on the side.

YELLOW SQUASH AND POTATO SOUP

Serves 4

A smooth, thick broth is poured over bits of browned potato in this rich, yet inexpensive, soup.

INGREDIENTS

2 Tbsp butter

½ cup chopped onion

1 garlic clove, minced

2 baking potatoes, cubed but not peeled

2–3 yellowneck squash, sliced

3 cups vegetable broth

Pinch of cayenne pepper

Pinch of ground black pepper

1 tsp paprika

½ tsp dried thyme

½ tsp dried basil

¾ cup light cream

Salt to taste

In a skillet over medium heat, melt the butter. Sauté the onion and garlic until wilted, about 5 minutes. Add the potatoes and sauté for 8 to 10 minutes. (You may need to add another tablespoon of butter at this point.) Remove 1 cup potatoes and keep warm. Add the squash to the skillet and sauté for about 3 minutes.

In a saucepan, mix together the broth and seasonings, then add the sautéed vegetables. Bring to a boil, then reduce the heat and simmer about 40 minutes. Purée the soup in batches in a blender or food processor.

Return the puréed soup to the saucepan and heat through. Add the cream and salt to taste and heat through but do not boil. Divide the reserved potatoes among serving bowls and ladle the soup over the potatoes.

PINZIMONIO

Serves 4

INGREDIENTS

1 red bell pepper, cut into strips

1 bulb sweet fennel, cut into strips and tossed lightly with lemon juice

1 Belgian endive, cut into spears

2–3 young artichoke hearts

½ cucumber, sliced

½–1 head radicchio, cored and leaves separated

4 celery stalks, cut into large pieces

Handful of arugula leaves

Sweet young carrots, blanched

4 ripe tomatoes, cut into wedges

Cruet of good fruity olive oil: allow 1–2 Tbsp per person

3–4 Tbsp balsamic vinegar per person

3–4 Tbsp flaked or coarse grain sea salt per person

1–2 Tbsp coarsely ground black pepper per person

1 lemon, cut into wedges

Cut the vegetables. Blanch the artichoke hearts if they have grown a choke and toss in lemon juice. Arrange the vegetables on a platter or in a basket. Diners at the table may want to chop their vegetables into pieces, so be sure to provide sharp knives.

Place the cruet of olive oil on the table. For each person, place a saucer of balsamic vinegar, a plate of salt, pepper, and lemon wedges on a plate so that they can mix their own sauce and vegetables.

TAMARILLO AND AVOCADO COCKTAIL

Serves 4

An excellent appetizer, with an interesting blend of flavors. The egg-shaped tamarillo fruit is native to South America and is also known as a "tree tomato." It has a tough, bitter skin that needs to be peeled, and reveals tart golden pink flesh that is purple-tinged around the seeds.

INGREDIENTS

3 tamarillos

Shredded lettuce

½ cup soft cheese with herbs and garlic

6 Tbsp Greek yogurt or sour cream

1 tsp superfine sugar

3 scallions or green onions, chopped

2 large ripe avocados

Peel the tamarillos thinly, halve them lengthwise, and slice across. Arrange a little shredded lettuce on 4 individual plates.

Mix the cheese with the yogurt or sour cream in a bowl. Sprinkle the superfine sugar over the tamarillos, mix in the chopped scallion, and leave to stand for 15 minutes.

Quarter and peel the avocados and slice them across.

Arrange the avocado slices on the lettuce, top with the tamarillo mixture, and spoon the cheese and yogurt dressing over the top.

CHEESE BELL PEPPERS

Serves 4

This is a simple but attractive idea. A slice from each of the red and green bell peppers makes a colorful appetizer.

INGREDIENTS

5½ oz mixed shelled nuts (peanuts, cashews, almonds, etc.)

Salt

Cayenne pepper

7 oz low-fat cream cheese

1 garlic clove, minced

Ground black pepper

1 medium red bell pepper

1 medium green bell pepper

Whole wheat toast, to serve

Heat a nonstick skillet over medium heat until evenly hot, then add the nuts, and cook until browned on all sides. Scatter some salt and cayenne pepper over some paper towels, add the hot nuts, and toss in the seasonings. Chop the nuts roughly when cooled.

Beat the cream cheese until smooth, then add the garlic and nuts. Season to taste with extra salt, if necessary, and black pepper. Cut the tops from the bell peppers and remove the seeds and cores. Pack the filling into the peppers, pressing it down firmly with the back of a spoon.

Chill the bell peppers for 2 to 3 hours before slicing. Serve one slice of each colored bell pepper to each person, with whole wheat toast.

MIXED VEGETABLE TAGINE

Serves 4

This dish can be made with raisins—you may like to add them when you make it—it's a matter of taste.

Serve the tagine *over couscous or rice.*

INGREDIENTS

¾ cup chickpeas, soaked overnight, then

drained and chopped

3 Tbsp olive oil

4 small carrots, sliced

2 chopped onions

3 garlic cloves, chopped

1 green bell pepper, sliced thin

2 sliced zucchini

1 tsp ground coriander

1 tsp ground cumin

3 tomatoes, chopped

2½ cups vegetable broth

Salt and pepper

Juice of 1 lemon

2 Tbsp fresh chopped parsley, to garnish

4 green onions, white part only,

chopped fine, to garnish

Cook the chickpeas in plenty of boiling water until just tender; the time will mainly depend on the age and variety of the chickpeas.

Meanwhile, heat the oil in a pan, add the carrots and fry until browned. Remove and reserve. Add the onion and garlic to the pan and cook gently until soft and golden. Add bell the pepper and zucchini and cook until softened. Stir in the spices and cook until fragrant, then add the tomatoes, carrots, broth, and seasoning. Bring to a boil.

Drain the chickpeas, add to the vegetable mixture, cover and simmer for about 30 minutes until all the vegetables are tender. Stir in the lemon juice, and sprinkle over the parsley and green onions.

BAKED TOMATOES

Makes 4 large or 8 small servings

Baked tomatoes are often regarded as a garnish rather than a serious vegetable dish. Here are some tips for making memorable baked tomatoes: Use tomatoes that are firm, not overripe. Time the cooking so you are ready to eat the tomatoes as soon as they come out of the oven. Make your own crisp bread crumbs by toasting good bread, and grinding it coarsely, rather than using bland, commercial breadcrumbs.

INGREDIENTS

4 large tomatoes, firm but ripe	⅔ cup dried bread crumbs
Salt	2 Tbsp chopped fresh basil or 2 tsp dried
2 Tbsp olive oil	2 Tbsp finely minced green onion
3 garlic cloves, minced	⅓ cup grated Parmesan cheese

Preheat a 425°F oven. Lightly grease a shallow baking pan. Core the tomatoes and cut them in half. Lightly salt the cut sides, and turn the tomatoes cut side down on paper towels to drain while you prepare the topping.

Heat the oil in a small pan. Add the garlic and sauté for 1 to 2 minutes, stirring and watching carefully so it doesn't scorch. If the oil is very hot, you may want to remove the pan from the burner. Add the bread crumbs, return pan to the heat, and cook 2 minutes, stirring almost constantly. Add the herbs and onion, continue cooking for about 30 seconds, and remove the pan from the heat. Stir in the Parmesan cheese.

Place the tomatoes, cut side up, on a lightly oiled baking pan. Divide the topping among tomatoes. Bake until the tomatoes lose their firmness but are not mushy, 15 to 20 minutes. Serve.

TORTILLA WHEELS WITH PINEAPPLE SALSA

Serves 8

Tortillas make excellent appetizers because they can be stuffed, sliced, and baked.
These tortilla wheels may also be served plain as finger food.

INGREDIENTS

For the filling

5¹/₂ oz cream cheese

1 green chile, seeded and chopped fine

2 Tbsp chopped fresh cilantro

4 tomatoes, seeded and chopped fine

4 scallions, chopped fine

1 bell pepper, red or yellow, seeded and chopped fine

3¹/₂ oz Cheddar cheese, shredded

Salt and ground black pepper

8 flour tortillas

For the salsa

1 Tbsp black mustard seeds

1 orange

4 thick slices pineapple, fresh or canned

1 small red onion, chopped fine

1 small green chile, seeded and chopped fine

2 tomatoes, diced

Salt and ground black pepper

Beat the cream cheese until smooth, then add all the other ingredients for the filling. Mix well and season to taste with salt and pepper. Divide the mixture among the tortillas, spreading it evenly. Place each tortilla on top of another, making four stacks of two, then roll them up tightly. Cover in plastic wrap and chill for at least 2 hours.

Prepare the salsa while the tortilla rolls are chilling. Heat a nonstick skillet until evenly hot, then add the mustard seeds, and cook for 1 to 2 minutes, until the seeds begin to pop. Allow to cool. Grate the rind from the orange, then peel it, and chop the flesh. Mix the orange with the mustard seeds and the other ingredients, seasoning to taste with salt and pepper. Allow the salsa to stand until required.

Preheat a 400°F oven. Unwrap the tortillas and trim away the ends, then cut each roll into eight slices. Place on baking sheets and bake in the preheated oven for 15 to 20 minutes, until well browned. Serve with the salsa.

LIGHT LUNCHES
AND SUPPERS

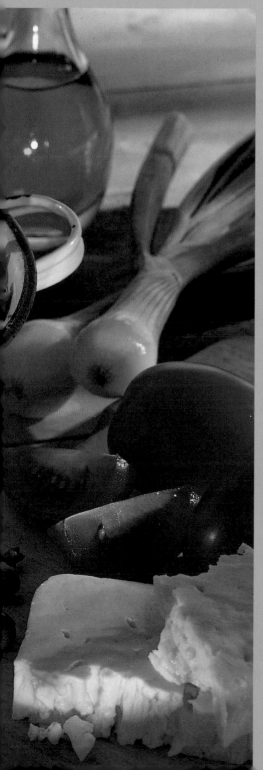

SPINACH CREPES

Serves 4

These light crêpes are made from a low-fat dough, and cook very quickly.

INGREDIENTS

For the crêpes

¾ cup all-purpose flour

½ cup water

1 tsp sunflower oil

For the filling

2 Tbsp vegetable broth

1 small zucchini, sliced

1 cup spinach, shredded

1 small onion, chopped

1 cup button mushrooms, sliced

½ red bell pepper, seeded

1 celery stalk, sliced

1 garlic clove, minced

Pinch of ground nutmeg

For the sauce

⅔ cup skim milk

1 Tbsp cornstarch

⅔ cup vegetable broth

Ground black pepper

1 Tbsp chopped fresh thyme

½ cup shredded vegetarian cheese

½ tsp paprika

Sift the flour for the crêpes into a mixing bowl and make a well in the center. Heat the water and oil to boiling point and pour into the flour, mixing to form a dough. Turn onto a floured surface and knead for 3 to 4 minutes.

Cut the mixture into four equal portions and roll each into a 6-inch round. Heat a heavy, nonstick skillet over medium heat. Put one of the crêpes into the pan and place another on top. Cook for 3 to 4 minutes, turning once when the bottom crêpe begins to brown. Repeat with remaining mixture. Cover and reserve.

Heat the broth for the filling in a saucepan and cook the vegetables, garlic, and nutmeg for 7 to 8 minutes, stirring. Drain the mixture well. Blend 2 tablespoons of the milk for the sauce to a paste with the cornstarch. Put in a saucepan with the remaining milk, vegetable broth, seasoning, thyme, and half of the cheese. Bring the mixture to a boil, stirring until thickened.

Heat a 375°F oven. Spoon the vegetable mixture onto one half of each crêpe and roll up. Put in a shallow ovenproof dish, seam side down. Pour the sauce over the top and sprinkle with the remaining cheese and paprika. Cook in the oven for 15 minutes until golden brown.

PASTA CAPONATA

Serves 4

Caponata is a well-known tomato and vegetable dish which is perfect to serve hot as a pasta sauce.
In this recipe dried penne have been used but any pasta shapes or noodles would work equally well.

INGREDIENTS

1 large eggplant

Salt

²/₃ cup vegetable broth

1 onion, halved and sliced

2 garlic cloves, minced

2 cups chopped plum tomatoes

2 Tbsp cider vinegar

4 celery stalks, chopped

2 oz green beans, trimmed

¹/₄ cup pitted green olives, halved

1 Tbsp chopped fresh basil

Ground black pepper

2 cups dried penne

Basil sprigs, to garnish

Cut the eggplant into chunks and put in a colander. Sprinkle with salt and let stand for 20 minutes. Wash under cold water and pat dry. Cook the eggplant under a medium broiler for 5 minutes, turning until browned.

Meanwhile, heat the broth in a saucepan and add the onion and garlic. Cook for 2 to 3 minutes until softened. Stir in the tomatoes, vinegar, celery, and beans. Cook over gentle heat for 20 minutes, stirring occasionally. Add the eggplant, olives, and basil, season, and cook for a further 10 minutes.

Meanwhile, cook the penne in boiling salted water for 8 to 10 minutes or until *al dente* (firm to the bite). Drain well and toss into the sauce. Spoon into a warmed serving dish, garnish with basil, and serve.

CHESTNUT HASH

Serves 4

Cook the potatoes for this dish in advance or use up any leftover cooked potatoes for speed.
Allow the potato to brown on the base of the pan for a crunchier texture.

INGREDIENTS

6 cups potatoes, peeled and cubed

1 red onion, halved and sliced

$\frac{1}{2}$ cup snow peas

$\frac{1}{2}$ cup broccoli florets

1 zucchini, sliced

1 green bell pepper, seeded and sliced

$\frac{1}{4}$ cup drained, canned corn kernels

2 garlic cloves, minced

1 tsp paprika

2 Tbsp chopped fresh parsley

1$\frac{1}{4}$ cups vegetable broth

$\frac{1}{3}$ cup chestnuts, cooked, peeled, and quartered

Ground black pepper

Parsley sprigs, to garnish

Cook the potatoes in boiling water for 20 minutes or until softened. Drain well and reserve.

Meanwhile, cook the remaining ingredients in a skillet for 10 minutes, stirring. Add the drained potatoes to the skillet and cook for 15 minutes more, stirring and pressing down with the back of a spoon. Serve immediately with bread.

VEGETABLE JAMBALAYA

Serves 4

This is a classic Caribbean dish, usually made with spicy sausage, but this vegetarian version packs just as much of a punch and tastes wonderful.

INGREDIENTS

Generous ¼ cup long grain white rice

¼ cup wild rice

1 eggplant, sliced and quartered

1 tsp salt

1 onion, chopped

1 celery stalk, trimmed and sliced

¾ cup vegetable broth

2 garlic cloves, minced

¾ cup baby corn

¾ cup green beans, trimmed

¾ cup baby carrots

1 cup canned chopped tomatoes

4 tsp tomato paste

1 tsp creole seasoning

1 tsp chili sauce

Chopped fresh parsley, to garnish

Cook the rices in boiling water for 20 minutes or until cooked. Drain well. Meanwhile, place the eggplant pieces in a colander, sprinkle with the salt, and leave to stand for 20 minutes. Wash and pat dry with paper towels.

Put the eggplant, onion, celery, and broth in a nonstick pan and cook for 5 minutes, stirring. Add the garlic, corn, beans, carrots, tomatoes, tomato paste, creole seasoning, and chili sauce. Bring the mixture to a boil, reduce the heat and cook for 20 minutes more until the vegetables are just cooked. Stir in the drained rice and cook for 5 minutes more. Garnish with parsley and serve.

GARLIC EGGPLANT ROLLS

Serves 8

These may take a little preparation but they are well worth the effort. Cooking garlic in its skin takes away the strong flavor and produces a milder garlic purée. This can be cooked in advance with the eggplant and gently warmed through to make the rolls.

INGREDIENTS

8 garlic cloves	2 Tbsp basil leaves, shredded
1 eggplant, sliced	4 lettuce leaves, shredded
1 Tbsp sunflower oil	4 ciabatta or large crusty rolls
½ cup sun-dried tomatoes, reconstituted	

Preheat a 400°F oven. Put the garlic and eggplant slices on a nonstick baking sheet and cook in the oven for 30 minutes until soft. Remove from the oven and cool.

Squeeze the garlic purée from the cloves, mix in with the sunflower oil, and reserve. Mix the sliced tomatoes, basil, and lettuce leaves together. Heat the rolls in a warm oven for 2 to 3 minutes and slice in half. Spread the garlic purée onto one half of each roll and top with the eggplant slices. Add the tomato mixture and top with remaining roll halves. Serve hot. Garnish with sliced tomatoes.

CHINESE NOODLES

Serves 4

This is a really quick and easy dish for a speedy lunch or supper. Use egg or rice noodles for a Chinese flavor or pasta ribbons if preferred, but these will require cooking for 8 to 10 minutes.

INGREDIENTS

8 oz thin egg or rice noodles	1 zucchini, sliced
⅓ cup vegetable broth	1 celery stalk, sliced
2 garlic cloves, minced	1 tsp curry powder
1 red onion, halved and sliced	3 Tbsp dark soy sauce
1-inch piece of ginger root, shredded	3 Tbsp plum sauce
1 red chile, chopped	1 tsp fennel seeds
2 carrots, cut into strips	Chopped fresh parsley or fennel leaves,
¾ cup snow peas	to garnish

Cook the noodles in boiling water for 3 minutes. Drain and reserve. Meanwhile, heat the broth in a nonstick wok or skillet and cook the vegetables and spices for 3 to 4 minutes, stirring constantly.

Add the drained noodles to the pan with the soy and plum sauces and the fennel seeds. Cook for 2 to 3 minutes, tossing well and serve garnished with parsley or fennel leaves.

CYPRIOT VILLAGE SALAD

Serves 4

A Cypriot salad contains many greens—caper stems; wild seaweed, lightly pickled; rocca (arugula); shredded cabbage (white, green, or red); purslane; and cilantro. You never know what greens will appear in your evening salad as the Cypriots are avid, daily hunters of wild herbs and salad leaves, and all of these go into their food. The only constant is the glistening, rich olive oil and the lemon halves plunked onto the table, to squeeze on as you like.

INGREDIENTS

½–1 small white cabbage, shredded	Extra virgin olive oil, as desired
Handful of arugula leaves, chopped	Juice of 1 lemon, plus extra lemon halves, to serve
3–4 Tbsp chopped fresh cilantro	
1–2 Tbsp chopped fresh parsley	Salt and black pepper to taste
Wild greens, optional (see above)	5–6 ripe, juicy tomatoes, quartered
1 cucumber, diced	10 or more black olives
1 bunch scallions, sliced thin	10 or more slightly bitter, green olives
Mint leaves, sliced thin (optional)	4 oz feta cheese, crumbled

Combine the cabbage, arugula, cilantro, parsley, wild greens (if using), cucumber, scallions, and mint. Toss with olive oil, lemon, salt and pepper, then arrange in a bowl.

Top with tomato wedges, black and green olives, and feta, and serve with more olive oil and lemon.

CUCUMBER TABBOULEH

Serves 6

A traditional tabbouleh is almost green in color from the high proportion of herbs to cracked wheat. It is important to dry the wheat thoroughly or the finished salad will be soggy and unpalatable.

INGREDIENTS

5½ oz fine cracked wheat or bulgur
⅔ cup boiling water
½ oz chopped fresh parsley
½ oz chopped fresh mint
2 tomatoes, seeded and chopped
2 scallions, trimmed and chopped fine
½ cucumber, diced
Juice of 1 lime
Salt and ground black pepper
2 fl oz fruity olive oil

Allow the cracked wheat to soak in the boiling water for 30 minutes then drain, if necessary, and squeeze dry in a clean dish towel.

Place the wheat in a large bowl and add all the remaining ingredients, including seasonings to taste. Toss the salad well and serve at room temperature.

Cypriot Village Salad ▶

EGGPLANT AND CHEESE PATE

Serves 6

A delicious creamy pâté to serve with toast or crackers.

INGREDIENTS

1 large or 2 small eggplants

1 cup cream cheese

1 garlic clove, minced

1 green chile, seeded and chopped

1 Tbsp tomato paste

Salt and ground black pepper

Paprika, to sprinkle

Cook the eggplant over a barbecue, under a broiler, or in a hot oven until the skin is wrinkled and blistered and the flesh is tender. Turn once or twice during cooking. Cover with a damp cloth and leave to cool for about 10 minutes, then peel off the skin.

Blend the eggplant with the remaining ingredients in a food processor or blender. Season well, then turn into a serving bowl. Sprinkle with paprika. Chill for 30 minutes before serving with hot toast or crusty bread.

BLUE CHEESE AND PECAN RISOTTO WITH SQUASH

Serves 4

A brilliant risotto, and so unusual! If you wish, use a piquant blue cheese such as English Stilton to give a tangy, sharp zing. However, a sweeter cheese, such as dolcelatte, will give a more subtle flavoring. The pecans are sweet and almost mystical in the slightly sticky rice.

INGREDIENTS

Good pinch of saffron threads

4 1/2 cups well-flavored vegetable broth

2 Tbsp olive oil

Knob of butter

1 onion, chopped fine

2 cups peeled, seeded, and diced squash, such as crown prince, acorn, or golden Hubbard

2 garlic cloves, minced

1 1/2 cups arborio rice

12 sage leaves, shredded

1 cup crumbled blue cheese

1 cup pecans, chopped

Salt and ground black pepper

Dressed arugula leaves, to garnish

Soak the saffron in the almost boiling broth until required—keep the broth as warm as possible. Heat the oil and butter together in a large skillet, then add the onion, and cook over low heat until softened but not browned.

Add the squash and cook quite quickly, until almost starting to brown, stirring all the time. Stir the garlic and the rice into the squash, and toss to coat in oil.

Add one third of the broth, then bring the rice to a boil, and cook, stirring frequently, until almost all the broth has been absorbed. Add half the remaining broth and repeat the cooking process, then add the sage leaves followed by the remaining broth. Continue cooking until almost all of the broth has been absorbed, then stir in the crumbled blue cheese and the chopped pecans.

Continue cooking until the cheese has just melted, then remove the pan from the heat, and season the mixture well, according to taste. Serve garnished with dressed arugula leaves.

EGGPLANT-STUFFED MUSHROOMS

Serves 4

Take the eggplant purée in advance for this recipe and store in the refrigerator for up to one day.

INGREDIENTS

1 eggplant	*1 Tbsp chopped fresh cilantro*
2 garlic cloves, minced	*8 large open cap mushrooms, peeled*
Juice of 1 lime	*¼ cup vegetarian cheese, shredded*
1 cup whole wheat bread crumbs	*4 Tbsp vegetable broth*
1 Tbsp tomato paste	*Cilantro sprigs, to garnish*

Heat a 425°F oven. Cut the eggplant in half lengthwise and place skin side uppermost in a baking dish. Cook in the oven for 30 minutes until soft. Remove the eggplant from the oven and allow to cool. Scoop the soft flesh from the skin and put in a food processor with the garlic and lime juice. Add the bread crumbs to the food processor with the tomato paste and cilantro and blend for 10 seconds to mix well.

Spoon the purée onto the mushrooms pressing the mixture down. Sprinkle the cheese on top and transfer the mushrooms to a shallow ovenproof dish. Pour the broth around the mushrooms, cover, and cook in the oven for 20 minutes. Remove the cover and cook for 5 minutes more until golden on top.

Remove the mushrooms from the oven and from the dish with a slotted spoon. Serve with a mixed salad and garnish with cilantro.

SQUASH-STUFFED ROASTED BELL PEPPERS

Serves 4

The combination of bell peppers and squash is a very happy culinary experience. Red bell peppers are much sweeter than green for baking or roasting; yellow are the next best.

INGREDIENTS

4 large red bell peppers	4 fresh tomatoes, skinned, halved, and seeded
4 cups peeled, seeded, and diced, firm-fleshed squash, such as crown prince, acorn, or kabocha	1¼ cups light cream
	½ cup shredded Parmesan cheese
2 large garlic cloves, sliced fine	Olive oil
Salt and ground black pepper	

Preheat a 425°F oven. Cut the bell peppers in half lengthwise—try to cut through the stalk and leave it in place as this will help to keep the bell peppers in shape. Remove the core and seeds, then rinse the bell peppers and arrange them in a suitable ovenproof dish or small roasting pan.

Pile the diced squash into the bell peppers, burying the sliced garlic in amongst the pieces. Season well, then top with the halved tomatoes.

Mix the cream with the Parmesan cheese and a little more seasoning, then carefully pour the mixture into the bell peppers.

Drizzle a little olive oil over, then bake at the top of the hot oven for 30 to 35 minutes, until the bell peppers are starting to blacken and the cheese is browned.

Serve hot, perhaps with fresh salad leaves or some stir-fried zucchini.

ROASTED VEGETABLES ON TOAST

Serves 4

The flavor of roasted vegetables is quite different than that achieved by boiling or steaming, and one not to be missed. This Mediterranean mixture is really colorful and tastes great with the light cheese sauce.

INGREDIENTS

1 fennel bulb, trimmed and quartered	**For the sauce**
2 open cap mushrooms, peeled and sliced	²/₃ cup vegetable broth
1 zucchini, sliced	¹/₃ cup skim milk
1 red bell pepper, halved, seeded, and sliced	2 garlic cloves, minced
	¹/₄ cup low-fat cream cheese
1 red onion, cut into eight pieces	Ground black pepper
1 Tbsp sunflower oil	1 tsp Dijon mustard
2 rosemary sprigs	1 Tbsp cornstarch
8 small slices of thick whole wheat bread	1 rosemary sprig, chopped
	Basil and rosemary sprigs, to garnish

Heat a 400°F oven. Blanch all of the vegetables in boiling water for 8 minutes and drain well. Transfer the vegetables to a roasting pan and sprinkle the oil and rosemary over the top. Cook in the oven for 25 minutes or until softened and beginning to char slightly.

Meanwhile, heat the broth for the sauce in a pan with the milk. Add the garlic, cream cheese, ground black pepper, and mustard. Blend the cornstarch with 2 tablespoons of cold water to form a paste and stir into the sauce. Bring to a boil, stirring until thickened and add the rosemary sprigs.

Cook the bread under the broiler for 2 to 3 minutes each side until golden. Arrange two slices of the toast on four warmed serving plates and top with the roasted vegetables. Spoon on the sauce, garnish with basil and rosemary, and serve immediately.

VEGETABLE ENCHILADAS

Serves 4

This is a vegetarian version of the Mexican dish.

INGREDIENTS

2 flour tortillas

For the filling

4 oz spinach, stems removed

4 scallions, sliced

$1/4$ cup shredded vegetarian cheddar cheese

Pinch of ground coriander

1 small celery stalk, trimmed and sliced

$1/3$ cup drained, canned corn kernels

1 carrot, peeled and shredded

For the sauce

$2/3$ cup skim milk

2 Tbsp cornstarch

$2/3$ cup vegetable broth

4 pickled jalapeño chiles, sliced

$1/2$ cup shredded vegetarian cheese

1 Tbsp tomato paste

1 Tbsp chopped basil

Basil or cilantro sprigs, to garnish

Blanch the spinach for the filling in boiling water for 2 to 3 minutes. Drain well and put in a mixing bowl with the scallions, cheese, coriander, celery, corn, and carrot.

Spoon half of the filling along one edge of each of the tortillas. Roll up the tortillas and cut in half. Put in a shallow ovenproof baking dish, seam side down.

To make the sauce, blend 4 tablespoons of the skim milk to a paste with the cornstarch. Heat the remaining milk and vegetable broth in a saucepan and stir in the cornstarch paste, jalapeño chiles, half of the cheese, and the tomato paste. Bring the sauce to a boil, stirring until thickened. Cook for 1 minute and pour over the tortillas in the dish.

Sprinkle the remaining cheese on top and cook in the oven at 350°F for 30 minutes or until the sauce is bubbling and the cheese has melted and is lightly golden. Garnish with basil or cilantro and serve with a small fresh salad.

VEGETARIAN CLASSICS

VEGETABLE AND TOFU PIE

Serves 8

In this recipe, firm tofu (bean curd) is cubed and added to the pie. If liked, use a marinated tofu for extra flavor and use in the same way.

INGREDIENTS

4 sheets of filo pastry	1 cup cauliflower florets
1 Tbsp polyunsaturated low-fat spread, melted	4 oz fine beans, halved
	2 celery stalks, sliced
	8 oz firm tofu, diced
For the filling	1¼ cups vegetable broth
1 leek, sliced	2 Tbsp chopped fresh cilantro
2 garlic cloves, minced	Ground black pepper
2 carrots, diced	1 Tbsp cornstarch

Place all the vegetables and tofu in a nonstick skillet and dry fry for 3 to 5 minutes, stirring. Add the broth and cilantro, season, and cook for 20 minutes or until the vegetables are tender. Blend the cornstarch to a smooth paste with 2 tablespoons of cold water, add to the mixture, and bring the mixture to a boil, stirring until thickened.

Spoon the mixture into an ovenproof pie dish. Lay one sheet of filo pastry on top and brush with melted fat. Cut the remaining pastry into strips and lay on top, folding as you go to create a rippled effect. Sprinkle the remaining fat on top and cook the pie in the oven at 400°F for 20 minutes until golden brown. Serve with new potatoes.

MIXED BEAN CHILI

Serves 4

Chili con carne has always been a warming favorite, and this recipe without the "carne" is no exception.
Packed with vegetables and beans, it is a fully satisfying meal.

INGREDIENTS

16 oz canned beans such as borlotti, red kidney, black-eyed, and pinto beans, drained

14 oz can chopped tomatoes

1 Tbsp tomato paste

1 onion, halved and sliced

²/₃ cup cubed potatoes

1 green bell pepper, seeded and chopped

³/₄ cup halved baby corn cobs

2 green chiles, seeded and chopped

1 tsp chili powder

2 garlic cloves, minced

²/₃ cup vegetable broth

Chopped fresh parsley, to garnish

Place all of the ingredients except the garnish in a large saucepan and bring to a boil. Reduce the heat, cover the pan, and simmer for 45 minutes or until all of the vegetables are cooked and the juices have thickened slightly. Stir the chili occasionally while cooking.

Garnish with parsley and serve with brown rice or baked potatoes.

VEGETABLE FLAN

Serves 4

This flan is made with low-fat pastry which is delicious hot when filled with vegetables and low-fat cheese.

INGREDIENTS

For the pastry

1 cup flour

2 Tbsp skim milk

1½ tsp baking powder

1 tsp mustard powder

For the filling

1 celery stalk, sliced

¾ cup button mushrooms, sliced

2 baby corn cobs, sliced

1 leek, sliced

2 garlic cloves, minced

8 asparagus spears, trimmed

½ cup vegetable broth

½ cup low-fat cottage cheese

⅔ cup skim milk

1 egg white, beaten

Preheat a 400°F oven. Mix the pastry ingredients in a bowl and add enough cold water to bring the mixture together to form a soft dough. Roll the pastry out onto a lightly floured surface to fit an 8-inch pie dish.

Cook the prepared vegetables in the broth for 5 minutes, stirring. Remove from the pan with a slotted spoon and place in a bowl. Add the cottage cheese, milk, and egg white. Spoon the mixture into the pastry case and cook for 40 minutes until set and golden brown. Serve hot with a fresh, crispy salad.

STUFFED PASTA SHELLS

Serves 4

INGREDIENTS

16 large pasta shells	**For the filling**
	4 Tbsp vegetable broth
For the sauce	1 zucchini, diced
16 oz can chopped tomatoes	$^{1}/_{4}$ cup canned or frozen corn kernels
2 garlic cloves, minced	1 green bell pepper, seeded and diced
1 Tbsp chopped fresh parsley	$^{3}/_{4}$ cup button mushrooms, sliced
1 onion, chopped	1 leek, sliced
2 Tbsp tomato paste	2 garlic cloves, minced
Ground black pepper	1 Tbsp chopped fresh mixed herbs
	Salt and ground black pepper
	Basil sprigs, to garnish

Place the sauce ingredients in a pan, bring to a boil, cover, and simmer for 10 minutes. Transfer to a food processor and blend for 10 seconds. Return the sauce to the pan and heat through. Meanwhile, put all of the filling ingredients, except the herbs, in a saucepan and cook for 10 minutes, simmering until the vegetables are tender. Stir in the herbs and season.

Cook the pasta in boiling salted water for 8 to 10 minutes until just tender, drain well. Spoon the vegetable filling into the pasta shells and arrange on warmed serving plates. Spoon the sauce around the shells, garnish with basil, and serve.

VEGETABLE CHOP SUEY

Serves 4

Add a touch of China to your table with this simple recipe.

INGREDIENTS

$1^{1}/_{4}$ cups vegetable broth	1 green bell pepper, seeded and cut into
1 tsp Chinese five spice powder	chunks
3 carrots, cut into strips	$^{1}/_{2}$ cup open cap mushrooms, sliced
3 celery stalks, sliced	3 cups bean sprouts
1 red onion, sliced	1 Tbsp light soy sauce

Pour the vegetable broth into a large skillet or wok with the Chinese five spice powder and cook all the vegetables except the mushrooms and bean sprouts for 5 minutes.

Add the mushrooms, bean sprouts, and soy sauce to the pan and cook for a further 5 minutes, stirring well. Serve immediately with boiled brown rice.

WILD RICE AND LENTIL CASSEROLE

Serves 4

This dish is superb on a cold day as it is really hearty and warming. To check that the rice is cooked, look at the ends to be sure they have split open, otherwise cook for a little longer until it is visibly cooked through.

INGREDIENTS

Scant 1 cup red split lentils

⅓ cup wild rice

4 cups vegetable broth

1 red onion, cut into eight pieces

2 garlic cloves, minced

14 oz can chopped tomatoes

1 tsp ground coriander

1 tsp ground cumin

1 tsp chili powder

Salt and ground black pepper

2½ cups button mushrooms, sliced

1 green bell pepper, seeded and sliced

1 cup broccoli florets

¾ cup halved baby corn cobs

1 Tbsp chopped fresh cilantro

Cilantro sprigs, to garnish

Cook the lentils and wild rice in the vegetable broth in a large flameproof casserole dish for 20 minutes, stirring occasionally.

Add the onion, garlic, tomatoes, spices, mushrooms, bell pepper, broccoli, and corn. Bring the mixture to a boil, reduce the heat, and cook for 15 minutes more until the rice and lentils are thoroughly cooked. Add the chopped cilantro, garnish, and serve immediately with warm crusty bread.

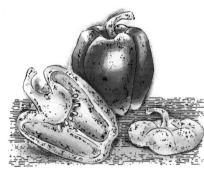

WINTER VEGETABLE CASSEROLE

Serves 4

This recipe makes use of many winter vegetables, but use whatever you have to hand as long as there is a good mixture. Cauliflower helps to thicken the sauce slightly, therefore it is always best to include this in your recipe.

INGREDIENTS

2 large potatoes, sliced

3¾ cups vegetable broth

2 carrots, cut into chunks

1 onion, sliced

2 garlic cloves, minced

2 parsnips, sliced

1 leek, sliced

2 celery stalks, sliced

1½ cups cauliflower florets

Salt and ground black pepper

1 tsp paprika

2 Tbsp chopped mixed herbs

¼ cup shredded vegetarian cheese

Cook the potatoes in boiling water for 10 minutes. Drain well and reserve. Meanwhile, heat 1¼ cups of the broth in a flameproof casserole dish. Add all of the vegetables, remaining broth, seasoning, and paprika, and cook for 15 minutes stirring occasionally. Add the herbs and adjust the seasoning.

Lay the potato slices on top of the vegetable mixture and sprinkle the cheese on top. Cook in the oven at 375°F for 30 minutes or until the top is golden brown and the cheese has melted. Serve with a fresh, crispy salad.

ROASTED PEPPER TART

Serves 8

This is one of those dishes that is as appealing to the eye as to the palate. A medley of roasted peppers in a cheese sauce are served in a crisp filo pastry shell. For a dinner party, make individual pastry shells and serve the tarts with a small salad.

INGREDIENTS

8 oz filo pastry

1 cup margarine, melted

For the filling

2 red bell peppers, halved and seeded

2 green bell peppers, halved and seeded

2 garlic cloves, minced

For the sauce

1¼ cups skim milk

¼ cup shredded vegetarian cheese

2 Tbsp cornstarch

¼ cup vegetable broth

1 Tbsp snipped fresh chives

1 Tbsp chopped fresh basil

1 garlic clove, minced

1 tsp whole grain mustard

Fresh basil and snipped chives, to garnish

Lay two sheets of filo pastry in a pie plate allowing the pastry to overhang the sides a little. Brush with margarine and lay another two sheets on top at opposing angles. Brush with margarine and continue in this way until all of the pastry has been used. Heat a 400°F oven and cook the pastry shell for 15 minutes until golden and crisp.

Meanwhile, lay the bell peppers on a baking sheet, skin side uppermost. Sprinkle the garlic over the bell peppers, cook in the oven for 20 minutes. Allow to cool slightly then peel the bell peppers, discarding the skin. Cut the bell peppers into strips and place in the pastry shell.

Heat the milk for the sauce in a pan, add the cheese, and stir until melted. Blend the cornstarch with 4 tablespoons cold water to form a paste and stir, with the broth, into the sauce. Bring to a boil, stirring until thickened and add the remaining ingredients. Spoon the sauce over the bell peppers, garnish with basil and chives, and serve.

PASTA TIMBALE

Serves 8

This is a really different way to serve pasta in a zucchini-lined mold which is baked until set and served with a tomato sauce.

INGREDIENTS

		For the sauce
2 zucchini	2 Tbsp drained, canned corn kernels	1 onion, chopped
1 cup pasta shapes such as macaroni or penne	1 green bell pepper, seeded and chopped	1 lb tomatoes, chopped
6 Tbsp vegetable broth	$^1/_4$ cup shredded vegetarian cheese	2 tsp granulated sugar
2 onions, chopped	16 oz can chopped tomatoes	2 Tbsp tomato paste
2 garlic cloves, minced	2 eggs, beaten	$^3/_4$ cup vegetable broth
1 carrot, chopped	2 Tbsp chopped fresh oregano	
	Salt and ground black pepper	

Cut the zucchini into thin strips with a vegetable peeler and blanch in boiling water for 2 to 3 minutes. Refresh the zucchini under cold water, then put in a bowl, and cover with cold water until required.

Cook the pasta in boiling salted water for 8 to 10 minutes until just tender. Drain well and reserve.

Heat the broth in a saucepan and cook the onions, garlic, carrot, corn, and bell peppers for 5 minutes. Stir in the pasta, cheese, tomatoes, eggs, and oregano, season well, and cook for 3 minutes, stirring well.

Line a 2-pint mold or round pan with the zucchini strips, covering the base and sides and allowing the strips to overhang the sides. Spoon the pasta mixture into the mold and fold the zucchini strips over the pasta to cover. Stand the mold in a roasting pan half filled with boiling water, cover, and cook in the oven at 350°F for 30 to 40 minutes until set.

Meanwhile, put all of the sauce ingredients in a pan and bring to a boil, then reduce the heat, and cook for 10 minutes more. Strain the sauce into a clean pan and heat gently.

Remove the pasta dish from the oven and carefully turn out of the mold onto a serving plate. Serve with the tomato sauce.

VEGETABLE GRATIN

Serves 4

INGREDIENTS

2 leeks, cut into strips lengthwise	¼ tsp freshly grated nutmeg
2 carrots, cut into sticks	⅔ cup apple juice
½ cup snow peas	⅔ cup vegetable broth
1 cup baby corn, halved	1 cup fresh white bread crumbs
2 garlic cloves, minced	2 Tbsp chopped fresh cilantro
1 Tbsp clear honey	¼ cup shredded low-fat cheese
½ tsp ground ginger	

Place the vegetables in a large pan of boiling water and cook for 10 minutes. Drain well and place in a shallow ovenproof dish. Mix together the garlic, honey, ginger, nutmeg, apple juice, and broth, and pour over the vegetables.

Mix together the bread crumbs and cilantro. Sprinkle over the vegetables to cover. Top with the cheese. Bake in the oven at 400°F for 45 minutes or until golden brown. Serve immediately.

TOFU BURGERS AND FRIES

Serves 4

Although not fries in the strictest sense, these potato sticks are baked to crispness in the oven.

INGREDIENTS

For the burgers

1 cup chopped carrots

½ cup shredded cabbage

1 onion, chopped

10 oz firm tofu (bean curd), cubed

1 tsp ground coriander

4 burger buns, split

Sliced tomatoes, lettuce, and onion

For the fries

2 large potatoes

2 Tbsp flour

1 Tbsp sunflower oil

Boil the carrots in water for 10 to 12 minutes until soft. Drain really well. Cook the cabbage in boiling water for 5 minutes and drain really well. Put the carrots, cabbage, onion, tofu, and coriander in a food processor and blend for 10 seconds. Using floured hands form the mixture into four equal-sized burgers. Chill in the refrigerator for 1 hour or until firm to the touch.

Cut the potatoes into thick fries and cook in boiling water for 10 minutes. Drain well and toss in the flour. Put the potatoes in a polythene bag and sprinkle in the oil. Seal the top of the bag and shake the fries to coat. Turn the potatoes out onto a nonstick baking sheet. Cook in the oven at 400°F for 30 minutes or until golden brown.

Meanwhile, place the burgers under a hot broiler for 7 to 8 minutes, turning with a spatula. Toast the burger buns for 2 minutes and place a burger on one half. Add the tomatoes, lettuce, and onion, top with the second half, and serve with the fries.

Vegetable Gratin ▶

VEGETABLE PILAF

Serves 4

A pilaf is a spicy, fluffy rice. This recipe is packed with crisp vegetables, chestnuts, and raisins and lightly colored with saffron for a golden appearance. If you do not have saffron to hand, use a pinch of turmeric in its place.

INGREDIENTS

2 Tbsp sunflower oil	2½ cups vegetable broth
1 red onion, chopped	½ cup cooked and peeled chestnuts,
¾ cup basmati rice	halved
Few strands of saffron	⅓ cup raisins
¼ cup corn kernels	
1 red bell pepper, seeded and diced	**For the sauce**
1 tsp curry powder	⅔ cup low-fat plain yogurt
1 tsp chili powder	2 Tbsp chopped fresh mint
1 green chile, seeded and chopped	Pinch of cayenne pepper
1 cup broccoli florets	

Heat the oil in a skillet and add the onion and rice. Cook for about 3 to 4 minutes, stirring. Add the remaining ingredients and bring the mixture to a boil. Reduce the heat and cook for 30 minutes more, stirring occasionally until the rice is cooked and the liquid absorbed.

Mix together the sauce ingredients and serve with the pilaf and a side salad.

POTATO AND CHEESE LAYER

Serves 4

This recipe uses half-fat cream substitute in place of full-fat cream. If preferred, substitute with skim milk or vegetable broth.

INGREDIENTS

1 lb potatoes, sliced thin

2 garlic cloves, minced

½ cup shredded cheese

1 onion, halved and sliced

2 Tbsp chopped fresh parsley

½ cup half-fat cream substitute   *1 cup half/half*

½ cup skim milk

Ground black pepper

Chopped fresh parsley, to garnish

Cook the potatoes in boiling water for 10 minutes. Drain well. Arrange a layer of potatoes in the base of a shallow ovenproof dish. Add a little garlic, cheese, onion, and parsley. Repeat the layers until all the potatoes, onion, cheese, garlic, and parsley are used, finishing with a layer of cheese.

Mix together the half-fat cream substitute and milk. Season and pour over the potato layers. Bake in the oven at 325°F for 1¼ hours until cooked through and golden brown. Sprinkle with black pepper, garnish with parsley, and serve.

SAFFRON, BELL PEPPER, AND MARSALA RISOTTO

Serves 4

This colorful and fragrant risotto has the added sweetness of peppers and Marsala wine.

INGREDIENTS

2 medium red bell peppers	2 Tbsp olive oil
2 medium yellow bell peppers	1 medium onion, chopped fine
2 medium green bell peppers	14 oz arborio rice
4 Tbsp Marsala wine	Large pinch of saffron
3½ cups vegetable broth	Salt and ground black pepper

Preheat a hot broiler. Halve and seed the bell peppers and place on a broiler. Cook for 7 to 8 minutes, turning occasionally, until the peppers are charred and softened. Carefully peel off the charred skin, then slice into thin strips. Place in a shallow bowl and mix in the Marsala wine. Set aside.

Pour the broth into a saucepan and bring to a boil. Reduce the heat to a gentle simmer. Meanwhile, heat the oil in a large saucepan and gently fry the onion for 2 to 3 minutes until just softened, but not browned. Add the rice and cook, stirring, for 2 minutes until well coated in the onion mixture. Add a ladleful of broth and cook gently, stirring, until absorbed. Continue ladling the broth into the rice until half the broth is used and the rice becomes creamy. Sprinkle in the saffron and seasoning.

Continue adding the broth until the risotto becomes thick and the rice is tender. This will take about 25 minutes and shouldn't be hurried. Stir in the bell pepper mixture and adjust seasoning before serving.

VEGETABLE LASAGNE

Serves 4

INGREDIENTS

1 small eggplant

Salt

16 oz can chopped tomatoes

2 garlic cloves, minced

1 Tbsp chopped fresh basil

1 large zucchini, chopped

1 onion, chopped

1 green bell pepper, seeded and chopped

1 cup button mushrooms, sliced

1 tsp chili powder

Ground black pepper

4 oz lasagne verdi (no precook variety)

For the sauce

$^2/_3$ cup vegetable broth

$1^1/_4$ cups skim milk

$^1/_2$ cup shredded vegetarian cheese

1 tsp Dijon mustard

2 Tbsp cornstarch

1 Tbsp chopped fresh basil

Slice the eggplant and put in a colander. Sprinkle with salt and leave for 30 minutes. Wash and pat dry. Put the tomatoes, garlic, basil, zucchini, onion, bell pepper, mushrooms, and chili powder in a saucepan. Add the eggplant, season, and cook for 30 minutes, stirring occasionally until the vegetables are cooked.

Mix the broth for the sauce, the milk, half of the cheese, and the mustard in a saucepan. Blend the cornstarch with 4 tablespoons cold water to form a paste and add to the pan. Bring to a boil, stirring until thickened.

Spoon a layer of the vegetable mixture into the base of an ovenproof dish. Lay half of the lasagne on top. Spoon on the remaining vegetable mixture and cover with the remaining lasagne. Pour the cheese sauce over the top and cook in the oven at 375°F for 40 minutes or until golden and bubbling. Sprinkle the basil on top and serve.

RATATOUILLE

Serves 4

A medley of vegetables cooked in a tomato and herb sauce. This is a strongly flavored dish to be served with a plainer recipe or used to top a baked potato.

INGREDIENTS

1 onion, halved and sliced

2 garlic cloves, minced

⅔ cup vegetable broth

1 large eggplant, sliced

6 oz zucchini, sliced

1 yellow bell pepper, seeded and sliced

2 Tbsp tomato paste

14 oz can chopped tomatoes

6 oz canned artichoke hearts, drained

2 Tbsp chopped fresh oregano

Ground black pepper

Place the onion, garlic, and broth in a skillet and cook for 5 minutes until the onion softens. Add the eggplant, zucchini, and yellow bell pepper and cook for a further 5 minutes.

Stir in the tomato paste, chopped tomatoes, artichoke hearts, and 1 tablespoon of the oregano. Season well. Bring to a boil, cover, and reduce the heat. Cook for 1 hour, stirring occasionally. Sprinkle with the remaining oregano and black pepper, and serve.

LENTIL MOUSSAKA

Serves 4–6

A meatless variation of the classic baked dish. This is rich, filling, and full of fiber, so it must be good for you!

INGREDIENTS

Olive oil, for frying

1 large onion, chopped

2 garlic cloves, minced

1 green bell pepper, cored and chopped

1 cup red lentils

About ⅔ cup red wine

2 cups canned chopped tomatoes

Salt and ground black pepper

1 Tbsp chopped fresh oregano

2 large eggplants, sliced

2½ cups milk

4 Tbsp butter, plus extra for greasing

4 Tbsp all-purpose flour

1 cup shredded Cheddar cheese

Preheat a 425°F oven. In a large pan heat 2 tablespoons of oil. Add the onion, garlic, and pepper and cook gently until soft. Add the lentils, red wine, and tomatoes. Bring to a boil, then season and add the oregano. Simmer for 20 minutes, or until the lentils are soft. Add a little more wine to the sauce if it seems dry.

Meanwhile, heat 2 to 3 tablespoons of oil in a skillet. Fry the eggplant slices on both sides until tender, adding more oil if necessary, then drain on paper towels. Add any oil left in the skillet to the lentil sauce.

Heat the milk, butter, and flour in a pan, stirring all the time, until boiling and thickened. Continue to cook for 1 minute, to remove the taste of flour from the sauce, then remove the pan from the heat. Add all but 2 tablespoons of the shredded cheese and then season to taste.

Layer the lentil sauce and eggplant slices in a buttered, ovenproof dish, finishing with a layer of eggplant. Spoon the sauce over the eggplants, then scatter the remaining cheese over the top. Bake in the preheated oven for 30 minutes, until the moussaka is browned and set. Serve with a salad and garlic bread.

SPICY GARBANZO BEANS

Serves 4

*Garbanzo beans are a great source of carbohydrate and are important in a vegetarian diet.
Here they are simmered in a spicy tomato sauce and are delicious served with brown rice.*

INGREDIENTS

1 cup garbanzo beans

1 tsp baking soda

1 onion, halved and sliced

1-inch piece of ginger root, shredded

4 tomatoes, chopped

1 green chile, chopped

1 tsp curry powder

½ tsp chili powder

1 tsp ground coriander

1¼ cups vegetable broth

Chopped fresh cilantro, to garnish

Put the garbanzo beans in a large mixing bowl with the baking soda and enough water to cover. Leave to soak overnight. Drain the garbanzo beans and cover with fresh water in a large saucepan. Bring to a boil and boil rapidly for 10 minutes. Reduce the heat and simmer for 1 hour or until cooked.

Drain the garbanzo beans and put in a nonstick skillet with the remaining ingredients. Cover and simmer for 20 minutes, stirring occasionally. Garnish with cilantro and serve with brown rice.

CREAMY MUSHROOM PASTA PIE

Serves 4

INGREDIENTS

1 lb puff pastry, thawed if frozen	Dash of olive oil	1½ oz all-purpose flour
Milk, to glaze	2 Tbsp butter	¼ pt skim milk
	1 garlic clove, minced	Salt and ground black pepper
For the filling	4 oz button mushrooms, sliced	3 oz mature Cheddar cheese, shredded
8 oz dried whole wheat pasta shells	12 baby corn cobs, cut into chunks	Freshly chopped parsley, to garnish

Preheat a 400°F oven. Roll the pastry out into two rectangular pieces, each measuring 6 x 4 inches. Set one rectangle aside to make the base of the pastry shell. Take the other piece and cut out an inner rectangle using a ruler and a sharp knife, leaving a 1-inch border to make the rim of the pastry shell. Reserve the inner rectangle to make the lid and, using a sharp knife, score it to make a pattern. Brush a little milk around the edges of the base of the pastry shell, and place the rim in position on top.

Place on a baking sheet with the lid alongside, and brush all the surfaces with milk to glaze. Bake for about 15 to 20 minutes, or until well risen and golden brown. Remove from the oven, and transfer the pastry shell to a wire rack to cool. If the center of the pastry shell has risen too high, gently press down to create a hollow space. Place on a serving plate.

To make the filling, bring a large saucepan of water to a boil and add the pasta shells with a dash of olive oil. Cook for 10 minutes, stirring occasionally, until tender. Drain well and set aside.

Melt the butter in a large saucepan, and sauté the garlic, mushrooms, and baby corn for 5 to 8 minutes, or until softened. Stir in the flour, and mix to form a paste. Gradually stir in the milk, a little at a time, stirring well after each addition. Bring the sauce slowly to a boil, stirring constantly to prevent lumps from forming. Season with salt and ground black pepper. Stir in the shredded cheese and continue to cook for a further 2 to 3 minutes, until the cheese has melted.

Stir the pasta into the sauce, then spoon the sauce into the pastry shell. Sprinkle with the chopped fresh parsley, then place the lid on top and serve.

PIZZA AND PASTA

BASIC PIZZA DOUGH

Makes two 12-inch thin crust pizzas or one deep-pan pizza

Basic pizza dough goes well with just about any topping you like.
This is the classic Italian base.

INGREDIENTS

1 package active dry yeast	2 Tbsp olive oil
1 cup warm water	½ tsp salt
5 cups unbleached white flour	

1. Combine the yeast, warm water, and 4 cups of the flour. Mix well to blend. Add the oil, salt, and remaining flour and work until the dough sticks together.

2. Place the dough on a lightly floured surface. Dust your hands with flour and knead the dough until it is smooth and elastic, about 5 minutes. If the dough gets sticky, sprinkle it with a little flour.

3. Roll the dough into a ball and place it in a lightly oiled bowl. Cover the bowl with a clean dish towel and set in a warm, but not hot place to rise until doubled in volume, about 1 hour.

4. When the dough has risen, roll it into a ball to make one deep-pan pizza or divide it in two balls to make two 12-inch thin crust pizzas. Before rolling out and topping the pizza, allow the dough to rest for 20 minutes.

5. When ready to bake, roll outward toward the edges with the palm of your hand until the dough fills the pan evenly.

PIZZA SAUCE

Makes about 2³/₄ cups sauce

Puréed tomatoes have the perfect consistency for pizza sauce. If you make extra sauce and freeze it, you'll always have some on hand.

INGREDIENTS

2 x 8-oz can puréed tomatoes	1 tsp dried basil
1 bay leaf	1 tsp dried thyme
1 tsp dried oregano	½ tsp dried marjoram

Place all the ingredients in a pan and bring to a boil. Reduce the heat, cover loosely to keep from spattering, and simmer for 30 minutes, stirring occasionally.

DEEP-PAN CREOLE PIZZA

Makes one 9 x 13-inch deep pan pizza

Creole dishes tend to be spicy tomato and vegetable mixtures, and this pizza is no exception.
Okra, or ladies' fingers, is available from many supermarkets. It exudes a sticky mucus when cut,
which adds a viscous texture to the topping.

INGREDIENTS

1 batch Basic Pizza Dough (see page 84)

8 oz okra

14-oz can chopped tomatoes

1 tsp dried oregano

1 tsp dried thyme

$^1/_2$ tsp dried basil

$^1/_2$ tsp cayenne pepper

2 garlic cloves, minced

2 celery stalks, chopped fine

1 small onion, chopped fine

Preheat a 500°F oven. Place the dough in the center of a lightly oiled 13 x 9 x 2-inch pan. Using your fingers, gently spread the dough until it covers the base of the pan evenly and goes halfway up the sides.

Boil the okra until tender then chop. Put the tomatoes into a colander, drain, and discard the liquid but retain the thick sauce. Place the tomatoes and sauce in a bowl. Add the herbs, cayenne pepper, and garlic. Add the celery and onions to the bowl. Finally, add the okra and stir gently to mix.

To assemble, spread the tomato and okra mixture onto the pizza dough and bake for 20 minutes.

PIZZA WITH CARAMELIZED ONIONS

Makes one 12-inch deep-pan pizza

Caramelized onions are cooked slowly in oil until they are golden brown and very soft. They have a wonderful flavor that goes well on a pizza. Make them ahead of time and store them in the refrigerator until ready to use.

INGREDIENTS

1 batch Basic Pizza Dough (see page 84)	2 tsp red wine vinegar
2 large onions	¾ cup Pizza Sauce (see page 84)
3 Tbsp olive oil	6 oz fontina cheese, shredded
½ tsp salt	

Preheat a 500°F oven. Slice both ends off the onions but do not peel. Cut the onions in quarters. Place them skin side down in a roasting pan. Liberally brush each onion with 1 tablespoon of the oil and sprinkle with salt. Cover the pan with aluminum foil and bake for 30 minutes. After 30 minutes, remove the foil and brush the onion with the remaining oil. Sprinkle with vinegar. Turn onion quarters on one side and return to the oven for 1 hour. Occasionally turn the onions and baste with the oil from the pan. When done, allow to cool or store in refrigerator for later use.

When ready to assemble the pizza, slice the onion quarters into strips. Spread the pizza sauce over the pizza dough. Spread sliced onion over the sauce and top with cheese. Bake for 10 minutes.

PIZZA WITH ROASTED PEPPERS

Makes one 12-inch deep-pan pizza

Roasting bell peppers enhances their flavor, and once you've tried them on pizza, they'll become a favorite.

INGREDIENTS

1 red bell pepper

1 green bell pepper

1 yellow bell pepper

³/₄ cup Pizza Sauce (see page 84)

3 oz fontina cheese, shredded1 batch

Basic Pizza Dough (see page 84)

Preheat a 500°F oven. Cut the tops off the bell peppers and remove the seeds. Cut the bell peppers in half and then squash them so that they lay relatively flat (it's okay if the edges rip). Place the bell peppers, skin side up, in a broiler pan and broil for about 8 minutes until blackened. Using tongs, place the bell peppers in a polythene bag. Seal and allow to cool. Once cooled, the skin will peel off easily. Discard the skins. Slice the roasted bell peppers into long strips.

Spread the pizza sauce on the pizza dough. Then decorate it with the bell pepper strips, alternating colors. There may be extra bell pepper strips, but cover them in olive oil, store in the refrigerator, and they'll keep for several days (use them on other pizzas or in salads). Lightly cover the bell peppers with the cheese. The cheese should not be so thick that the colorful peppers are obscured. Bake for 10 minutes.

PIZZA PAELLA

Makes one 12-inch deep-pan pizza

In this vegetarian version of classic Spanish paella, leeks replace the fish and meat.
But it retains the traditional flavoring of saffron, garlic, and onions.

INGREDIENTS

2 leeks	½ tsp salt
2 Tbsp olive oil	½ tsp cayenne pepper
1½ onions, chopped rough	1½ cups frozen peas, thawed
2 large garlic cloves, minced	2–3 Italian plum tomatoes, chopped
1 Tbsp lemon zest, cut in strips	1 batch Basic Pizza Dough (see page 84)
Large pinch of saffron	2¼-oz jar sliced black olives, drained

Preheat a 500°F oven. Chop the leeks into 1-inch pieces. Heat the oil in a pan over medium heat and add the onions, leeks, garlic, lemon rind, saffron, salt, and cayenne pepper. Sauté for 5 minutes, stirring frequently.

Remove from the heat and stir in the peas and tomatoes. Spread the mixture on the pizza dough. Top with the drained olives. Bake for 10 minutes.

INDIVIDUAL PESTO PIZZAS

Makes four 6-inch pizzas

Homemade pesto is so good it's worth growing a crop of basil in your garden in order to have easy access. These pizzas make great appetizers, but are also good as the main course for lunch.

INGREDIENTS

	For the pesto sauce
4 pieces of pita bread (6-inch diameter)	
1 small red onion, sliced thin	½ cup fresh basil leaves, no stems
1 small Roma tomato, sliced thin	1 Tbsp pine nuts
4 oz mozzarella cheese, sliced	1 large garlic clove, minced
	¼ cup extra virgin olive oil
	¼ cup Parmesan cheese

First make the pesto sauce. Put the basil, pine nuts, garlic, olive oil, and Parmesan cheese in a blender or food processor and mix until thoroughly blended. Make ahead of time and refrigerate if you wish.

To make the pizza, toast the pita bread. Then top each piece with 1 tablespoon of pesto sauce, a slice of onion, a slice of tomato, and finally, a slice of mozzarella cheese.

Pizza Paella ▶

MINI COCKTAIL PIZZAS

Makes 8 mini pizzas

Use muffins as the recipe suggests, or a prebaked base cut into small circles.

These simple pizzas are pretty to look at as well as tasty to eat.

INGREDIENTS

4 muffins, halved

¹/₂ cup Pizza Sauce (see page 84)

4 oz Gruyère cheese, shredded

1 medium ripe tomato

2 tsp olive oil

4 tsp chopped fresh parsley

Lightly toast the muffin halves. Then spread pizza sauce on each muffin half. Top with the cheese. Broil for 5 minutes, or until the cheese is bubbly and begins to turn golden brown.

Slice the tomato in thin, perfect rounds. Top each broiled muffin with one tomato slice. Brush with a little olive oil and sprinkle with about ¹/₂ teaspoon of parsley. Serve immediately.

SPINACH AND WALNUT MINI PIZZAS

Makes 12 mini pizzas

Walnut oil makes an unusual vinaigrette for this pizza. Choose a good-quality

Gorgonzola for the tangy, creamy topping.

INGREDIENTS

¹/₂ cup walnut oil

1 cup walnut halves, broken

2 Tbsp red wine vinegar

¹/₂ tsp salt

2 green onions, chopped fine

6 muffins, halved

4 oz fresh spinach, stems removed

6 oz Gorgonzola cheese

Pour the oil over the walnuts and marinate for about 15 minutes. Strain the walnuts and set aside. Mix the vinegar, salt, and green onions into the oil.

Lightly toast the muffin halves. Wash the spinach and remove the stems. Pat dry

and place about three leaves on each of the toasted muffins. Top with a scant tablespoon of the dressing, 1 tablespoon of walnuts, and top with the cheese. Place under the broiler for about 3 minutes until the cheese begins to melt.

◀ *Mini Cocktail Pizzas*

TOMATO AND MUSHROOM PIZZA

Serves 4

Tomatoes and mushrooms have a natural affinity. This pizza topping creates a wonderfully deep and rich flavor, which is lifted by the inclusion of fresh oregano.

INGREDIENTS

1 batch Basic Pizza Dough (see page 84)	8 oz common cultivated mushrooms, white or brown, sliced thin
4 Tbsp tomato paste (optional)	
½ cup puréed tomatoes	12 oz mozzarella cheese, or half mozzarella, half fontina, shredded
2–3 fresh ripe or canned tomatoes, diced	
	2 Tbsp olive oil
1 garlic cloves, minced	Freshly shredded Parmesan cheese, to taste
1 tsp fresh oregano, crumbled	

Preheat a 400°F oven. Roll out the dough and use to line an oiled pizza pan. Spread the dough with the tomato paste, if using, then drizzle with the puréed tomatoes. Scatter the tomatoes, garlic, oregano, mushrooms, and mozzarella cheese, or mozzarella and fontina cheeses, over the top. Drizzle with the olive oil, and sprinkle Parmesan cheese.

Bake in the oven for 15 to 20 minutes, or until the cheeses have melted and the crust is golden.

CHEESE AND ARTICHOKE PIZZA

Makes one 12-inch double-crust pizza

Artichoke hearts bottled in olive oil are already marinated. Assemble the ingredients and bake them to produce a quick and perfectly seasoned pizza.

INGREDIENTS

1 batch Basic Pizza Dough (see page 84)

10-oz bottle artichoke hearts

⅔ cup shredded mozzarella cheese

⅔ cup grated fresh Romano cheese

2 garlic cloves, minced

2-oz jar sliced pimentos, drained

Preheat a 500°F oven. Drain the artichoke hearts, reserving the liquid. Finely chop the artichoke and place in a bowl. Add both cheeses, garlic, and drained pimentos. Measure ¼ cup of the reserved liquid from the artichoke hearts and add it to the bowl. Stir to mix.

Top the pizza dough with the artichoke and cheese mixture and bake for 10 minutes, until the cheese is melted and golden.

Tomato and Mushroom Pizza ▶

PENNE AI FUNGHI

Serves 4

Sautéed mushrooms and asparagus pieces, simmered in a tomato-cream sauce, then tossed with quill-shaped penne and fresh basil, make a flavorful, rich Italian pasta.

INGREDIENTS

1 onion, chopped rough

4 garlic cloves, chopped rough

3 Tbsp olive oil or butter, plus a little extra to finish

12 oz mixed mushrooms, cut into bite-sized pieces

Salt and ground black pepper

1 lb fresh tomatoes, chopped fine, or 8 oz canned chopped tomatoes in their juice

$\frac{1}{4}$–$\frac{1}{2}$ tsp sugar

1$\frac{1}{2}$ cups heavy cream

1–2 oz fresh sweet basil, torn

12–16 oz fresh penne

1 bunch thin asparagus, tough ends broken off, cut into bite-sized lengths

4–6 Tbsp shredded Parmesan cheese

Sauté the onion and garlic in the olive oil or butter, until softened and almost transparent. Then add the mushrooms and cook, stirring occasionally to prevent sticking. Season with salt and pepper, then pour in the tomatoes, and add the sugar. Bring to a boil and cook, stirring, a few minutes more. Then add the cream and about a third of the fresh basil. Taste, adjust the seasoning if necessary, and remove from the heat.

Cook the pasta in a large pan of boiling salted water until half done, then add the asparagus, and finish cooking. The pasta should be *al dente* (firm to the bite) and the vegetables just tender. Drain well.

Toss the hot pasta and asparagus with the creamy tomato-mushroom sauce, then toss with the Parmesan cheese, remaining basil, and a little extra olive oil or butter. Serve while piping hot on warmed plates with fresh crusty bread.

TOMATO SPAGHETTI WITH MUSHROOMS

Serves 4–6

For this dish you need to include at least one kind of dried mushroom as this will give the depth of flavor that is so typical of Italian mushroom-based dishes. Dried porcini keep well, and are an ingredient that no well-stocked kitchen should be without.

INGREDIENTS

For the sauce

½ oz dried porcini mushrooms

3 Tbsp olive oil

1 red onion, peeled and cut into wedges

3–6 smoked or regular garlic cloves, thinly sliced

4 oz mushrooms, such as oyster or chanterelle, wiped and sliced

4 oz button mushrooms, wiped and sliced

6 Tbsp red wine

2 Tbsp extra virgin olive oil

Salt and ground black pepper

2 Tbsp chopped fresh sage

To serve

1 lb fresh tomato spaghetti

Chopped fresh sage

Soak the porcini in warm water for about 20 minutes. Drain, reserving the soaking liquid, and chop the porcini. Heat the oil in a pan and sauté the onion and garlic for 3 minutes. Add the chopped porcini, oyster or chanterelle, and button mushrooms. Sauté for a further 5 minutes, stirring frequently.

Strain the porcini soaking liquid into the pan and add the red wine. Bring to a boil, then simmer for 5 minutes or until the mushrooms are just cooked and the liquid has been reduced by about half. Stir in the extra virgin oil, season to taste, and add the sage. Cover with the lid, remove from the heat, and reserve.

Meanwhile, cook the tomato spaghetti in plenty of boiling salted water for 3 to 4 minutes or until *al dente*. Drain and return to the pan. Add the mushrooms and sauce, and toss the ingredients lightly. Serve, garnished with the chopped fresh sage.

PASTA WITH SUN-DRIED TOMATO SALSA

Serves 4

The intense flavors of this powerful salsa may clash in concentrated form. When it is tossed with pasta, however, the flavors blend and become complementary.

INGREDIENTS

3 Tbsp olive oil	1 Tbsp chopped fresh basil
6 garlic cloves, minced	4 bacon slices, cooked and crumbled
1 tsp dried chiles	2 oz sliced black olives
1 red bell pepper, cored, seeded, and cut into quarters	12 oz–1 lb pasta
	Grated Parmesan cheese
4 oz sun-dried tomatoes, packed in oil	

Heat the oil in a small frying pan over low heat. Add the garlic and the dried chiles. Cook slowly, stirring often and pressing the garlic to release the juices, until the garlic is lightly browned, 5 to 8 minutes. The heat must be very low or the garlic may scorch and turn bitter. Remove from the heat and let stand while you prepare the other ingredients.

Cook the red bell pepper skin side down over a barbecue fire or skin side up under a broiler until the skin is blackened. Remove from the heat and place it in a polythene bag to steam for 10 minutes. Peel off the skin and chop the flesh.

Chop the sun-dried tomatoes and put them into a small bowl with the basil. Add the bacon, garlic–chili–olive oil mixture, red bell pepper, and sliced olives. Cook the pasta in plenty of boiling salted water until just tender or *al dente*. Drain well, and then toss with the salsa and Parmesan cheese.

PASTA WITH ZUCCHINI, RICOTTA, AND WALNUTS

Serves 4

A classic dish from Liguria, Italy, the richness of the nuts and the bland, milky,
ricotta cheese are enhanced by the smooth fragrance of the olive oil.

INGREDIENTS

1 lb pappardelle

4–6 zucchini, sliced

4–6 garlic cloves, chopped

4 Tbsp extra virgin olive oil

1 cup ricotta cheese, crumbled

1–1½ cups shredded sharp cheese

¼ cup or a generous handful of walnuts,
chopped into pieces

1–2 tsp fresh thyme leaves

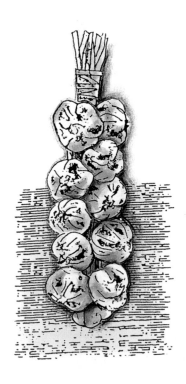

Cook the pasta in rapidly boiling water for five minutes, then add the zucchini and continue cooking until *al dente*. Drain.

Toss the hot, cooked, drained pasta and zucchini with the garlic, olive oil, ricotta and shredded cheeses, walnuts, and thyme. Serve immediately.

WARM PASTA SALAD

Serves 4

This salad combines the saltiness of green olives, the crunch of walnuts, and the goodness of fresh vegetables. Use freshly shredded Parmesan cheese, not the packaged kind; you'll notice a big difference in flavor. The flavors are enhanced when this salad is served warm, but if you have any cold leftovers, add a splash of vinaigrette.

INGREDIENTS

8 oz fusilli or other pasta	*½ small zucchini, sliced thin*
6 asparagus spears	*2 green onions, chopped*
3 Tbsp extra virgin olive oil	*½ cup walnut pieces*
⅓ cup shredded Parmesan cheese, plus extra for topping	*⅓ cup green olives, quartered*
	Salt and ground black pepper

Cook pasta according to the directions on the package. While the pasta is cooking, blanch the asparagus for 2 to 3 minutes in boiling water. Drain and cut into 1-inch pieces.

When the pasta is cooked, drain but do not rinse, then put it in a large mixing bowl. Pour the olive oil over the pasta, and toss with two forks. Add the Parmesan, and toss again. Stir in the asparagus, zucchini, green onions, walnuts, and green olives. Add salt and pepper to taste. Serve with a sprinkling of Parmesan over the top.

SPAGHETTI WITH BROCCOLI AND PISTOU

Serves 4

Broccoli, cooked with garlic, tomatoes, and olive oil, is tossed with spaghetti, then served with a generous scoop of pistou—a delicious mixture of crushed basil, garlic, and olive oil; a French version of Italy's pesto. It is a deliciously hearty dish from the Italian coast of Liguria.

INGREDIENTS

1 bunch broccoli, cut into bite-sized pieces and florets

3–4 garlic cloves, chopped

4–5 Tbsp extra virgin olive oil

Pinch of crushed, dried red chili pepper (or chili flames)

2 cups/14 oz canned tomatoes with the juice, or fresh tomatoes

1 Tbsp tomato paste, if using fresh tomatoes

Sea salt to taste

12 oz spaghetti

3–5 Tbsp pistou

Blanch the broccoli until crisp-tender, then drain, and place in a skillet with the garlic, olive oil, and chili over a medium-high heat. Cook for a minute or two, then add the tomatoes, tomato paste, and sea salt, and cook for a few minutes over high heat.

Cook the spaghetti until *al dente*, then drain, and toss with the hot broccoli and tomato sauce. Serve each portion with a generous scoop of pistou.

SPICY VEGETABLE DISHES

SPICY GREEN BEANS

Serves 3–4

Marinate these beans early in the day, and you'll have a spicy dish by dinner. These make an easy and convenient addition to a picnic or tailgate party.

INGREDIENTS

1 lb fresh green beans, topped and tailed

2 Tbsp vegetable oil

2 Tbsp white wine vinegar

1 Tbsp freshly squeezed lemon juice

1 tsp Creole mustard

1 garlic clove, minced

1 green onion, minced

1 tsp chili-pepper flakes

¼ tsp salt

Cook the green beans in boiling water until just tender, 3 to 4 minutes. Drain and plunge into cold water, then drain well again. In a glass or other nonreactive dish, whisk together all the remaining ingredients. Add the beans and stir to coat thoroughly. Refrigerate for at least 3 hours. Serve chilled.

PAPRIKA POTATO SALAD

Serves 4

This salad has a spicy Indian flavor. Perfect served accompanying either a spiced main dish or a green salad.

INGREDIENTS

1 lb potatoes

½ cup vegetable broth

1 red onion, halved and sliced

¼ tsp ground cumin

1 green chile, chopped

¼ tsp ground turmeric

1 cardamom pod

1 tsp paprika

1 tomato, seeded and diced

1 Tbsp chopped fresh parsley

Cut the potatoes into 1-inch cubes. Cook in boiling water for 10 minutes. Drain well and reserve.

Heat 3 tablespoons of the broth in a pan, add the onion and cook for 5 minutes until beginning to brown. Add the potatoes, cumin, chile, turmeric, cardamom pod, and paprika. Stir in the remaining broth and the tomato. Bring to a boil and cook for 5 minutes. Remove the cardamom pod, sprinkle with parsley, and serve.

SPICED EGGPLANT

Serves 4

An Indian eggplant dish which is perfect with curry or a plain vegetable casserole.
Spicy in itself, it is also delicious cold as an appetizer.

INGREDIENTS

1 lb eggplant	½ tsp curry powder
6 oz potatoes	3 garlic cloves, minced
4 Tbsp vegetable broth	1 tsp chili powder
½ onion, sliced	Pinch of ground turmeric
1 small red bell pepper, seeded and diced	Pinch of sugar
¼ tsp ground coriander	1 green chile, diced
¼ tsp ground cumin	1 Tbsp chopped fresh cilantro
1 tsp shredded ginger	

Dice the eggplant into small cubes. Cut the potatoes into 1-inch chunks. Heat the broth in a pan, add the onion, and cook for 2 to 3 minutes. Stir in the red bell pepper, ground coriander, cumin, ginger, curry powder, garlic, chili powder, and turmeric, and cook for 2 to 3 minutes.

Add the eggplant, sugar, green chile, and ⅔ cup water, cover, and simmer for 15 minutes. Add the potato, re-cover, and cook for 10 minutes. Stir in the fresh cilantro and serve.

HARISSA

Makes 1 cup

Or "arhissa" as it is sometimes called, is a fiery paste based on chiles. It is primarily associated with Tunisia but it is also used in Algeria and Morocco. As well as being served as a condiment at the table, in a small dish with a small spoon, Harissa is used in cooking to add life to meat, poultry, or vegetable casseroles, saffron-flavored fish soups and stews, "stewed" red bell peppers, and tomatoes. It is often used as a base for poached eggs, or added to dips, sauces, and salad dressings.

INGREDIENTS

2 oz dried red chiles, soaked in hot water
for 1 hour

2 garlic cloves, chopped

2 tsp coriander seeds

2 tsp cumin seeds

2 tsp caraway seeds

Pinch of salt

6 Tbsp olive oil

Drain the chiles and put in a mortar, spice grinder, or small blender with the garlic, spices, and salt. Mix to a paste then stir in 3 tablespoons of olive oil. Transfer to a small jar and pour a little oil over the surface. Cover and keep in the refrigerator for up to two days.

SPICED POTATO CAKES

Serves 4–6

These tasty fried potato cakes come from Algeria. The spicy mashed potato
mixture is also good served simply as it is.

INGREDIENTS

2 lb mashed potato

1 Tbsp paprika

2 tsp ground cumin

Good pinch of cayenne pepper

1 bunch of cilantro, chopped

3 eggs

Salt and ground black pepper

Oil, for frying

In a large bowl, mix the potato with the spices, cilantro, eggs, and seasoning. With floured hands, form the mixture into round flat cakes. Cover and refrigerate for 30 minutes.

Heat a shallow layer of oil in a large frying pan, add the cakes in batches, and fry until crisp and golden brown on both sides. Transfer to paper towels to drain any excess oil. Serve hot.

SPICED PARSNIPS

Serves 4–6

This version of Tunisian Mzoura *is sweet and spicy, and made as hot as you like with*
Harissa. *It is also made, more traditionally, with carrots.*

INGREDIENTS

2 lb small parsnips, sliced

3 Tbsp olive oil

1 small onion, chopped fine

1 garlic clove, chopped fine

1 tsp Harissa (see page 107)

1 tsp ground cumin

1 tsp ground coriander

1 tsp clear honey

⅔ cup vegetable broth

Salt and ground black pepper

Chopped cilantro, to garnish

Cook the parsnips in a saucepan of boiling water for about 7 minutes, then drain. Meanwhile, heat the oil in a frying pan, then add the onion and garlic and cook gently until softened. Stir in the *Harissa* and spices, then add the honey, broth, parsnips, and seasoning. Cook for 7 to 10 minutes, until the parsnips are tender and the liquid reduced to a sauce. Serve hot or cold sprinkled with cilantro.

Spiced Potato Cakes ▶

SPICED GLAZED CARROTS WITH DILL WEED

Serves 4

Dill weed, ginger, and orange produce this distinctive dish. Shake the pan toward the ends of cooking to prevent the carrots from sticking.

INGREDIENTS

1 lb carrots, cut into thin sticks

¹/₂ stick butter

1 Tbsp sugar

¹/₂-inch piece of gingerroot, shredded

Thickly grated rind of 1 orange

Salt and ground black pepper

Few sprigs of dill weed, chopped

Put the carrots, butter, sugar, ginger, orange rind, and seasoning in a pan and just cover with water. Bring to a boil then simmer for about 12 minutes until the carrots are tender and the liquid has evaporated. Garnish with the dill weed.

FRIED BELL PEPPERS WITH CAPERS AND GARLIC

Serves 4–6

The essential character of this bell pepper dish comes from the slightly charred taste of the bell peppers which are fried until their skins are scorched. The dish can be served hot as a vegetable accompaniment, or chilled as an appetizer.

INGREDIENTS

4 Tbsp olive oil

1¾ lb red bell peppers, cut into strips

4 garlic cloves, sliced

1 Tbsp salt-packed capers

2 Tbsp white wine vinegar

Salt and ground black pepper

Heat the oil in a frying pan until it is quite hot, then fry the bell peppers, stirring frequently, until they are charred around the edges. Add the garlic and capers. Cook until they sizzle, then stir in the vinegar and seasoning; because of the salt in the capers a little additional salt will be necessary.

Allow the vinegar to evaporate for a minute or so, then either serve immediately, or allow to cool, cover, chill, and serve cold.

POLENTA WITH BLACK-EYED PEA SALSA

Serves 6

This is a hybrid dish, combining Italian polenta with Southwestern black-eyed pea salsa. The polenta must be prepared in advance. Traditional polenta—a coarse grind of cornmeal—needs cooking for at least 30 minutes, but now quick-cooking polentas are available; however, they taste better if you cook them for 10 minutes longer than recommended on the package.

INGREDIENTS

Polenta (recipe follows)

Olive oil for frying or broiling

12 oz Cheddar cheese, sliced thin

9 oz black-eyed pea salsa (purchased salsa mixed with black-eyed peas)

INGREDIENTS FOR POLENTA

2 tsp salt

10 oz polenta

Lightly oil a loaf pan, about 9 x 5 inches. Bring 5½ cups water and the salt to a boil in a large saucepan. Slowly add the polenta, stirring constantly and watching for lumps. Cook over low heat, stirring almost constantly, 30 minutes or so, until the polenta forms a thick mass that pulls cleanly away from the sides of pan. Pour the polenta into the loaf pan and smooth the top. Allow to cool for at least 30 minutes before turning the set mixture out.

Cut the polenta into slices about 1½ inches thick. If you are going to barbecue it, lightly brush the cut edges with olive oil. If you are going to fry it, heat 1 tablespoon olive oil in a pan.

When the oil is hot, or when the barbecue coals are glowing and the flames have died, put the polenta slices on the heat. Cook until the bottom is golden (if frying) or charred with grid marks, about 3 minutes. Turn the polenta and put the sliced cheese on top. Cook until the underneath is golden or charred. (Note: If you are frying the polenta, the cheese will melt more readily if you use a lid on the pan. Add more oil if necessary before frying the next batch of polenta.)

Remove the polenta from the heat. Spoon black-eyed pea salsa over the top, and serve.

EGGPLANT AND SWEET POTATO CURRY

Serves 4

This makes a substantial main course, but it could also be served as a side dish with curries.

INGREDIENTS

2 tsp cumin seeds

1 Tbsp mustard seeds

3 Tbsp ghee or sunflower oil

2 small sweet potatoes, about 1 lb,
peeled and cut into ½-inch chunks

1 large onion, sliced fine

2 garlic cloves, sliced

1–2 tsp chili powder

1 tsp ground turmeric

1 large eggplant, cut the same size as the
potato

1 Tbsp blue poppy seeds

1 cup water or vegetable broth

2 tsp salt

1 Tbsp torn fresh cilantro leaves

Heat a large skillet over medium heat, then add the cumin and mustard seeds and dry-fry for 30 seconds or so, until aromatic and starting to pop. Transfer to a plate and leave to cool. Heat the ghee or oil in the pan, add the potatoes and cook for 3 to 4 minutes until starting to soften. Add the onion, garlic, chili powder, and turmeric, and cook for 1 to 2 minutes, then add the eggplant with the roasted spices and the poppy seeds. Stir in the water and salt, then cover and simmer slowly for 30 to 45 minutes, until the vegetables are tender.

Season the curry to taste, then serve sprinkled with the cilantro.

ROASTED CORN

Serves 6

It's hard to improve on corn when it is fresh-picked, sweet, and tender. This recipe uses butter that has been seasoned with fresh chives and paprika, but you can substitute other fresh herbs and spices to suit your taste—basil, oregano, cumin, cayenne pepper, and chili powder all work well. Or brush the corn with garlic-flavored olive oil.

INGREDIENTS

6 ears of corn, husks on

½ cup butter, softened to room
temperature

2 Tbsp minced fresh chives

1 tsp paprika

Mound a pyramid of coals in the center of the barbecue, set alight, and leave to heat up.

Pull down the corn husks but don't remove them. Remove the silks and rinse the corn. Wipe the corn dry. If your grocer has already removed all or part of the husks, you can use aluminum foil instead.

Put the softened butter in a small bowl with the chives and paprika. Mash the butter with a fork until the chives and paprika are well mixed into it. Spread a scant amount of butter on each ear of corn. You don't want to use more than half the butter on this step. If you do, make more seasoned butter to serve on the side. Pull the husks back up so all the corn is covered. If there are no husks or if they have been trimmed to expose part of the corn, wrap each ear in foil.

When the barbecue flames have died and the coals are glowing and covered with ash, put the corn around the edges of the grill, not over the coals. Cover the barbecue. Cook the corn 20 minutes if it is young and tender, 25 minutes if the kernels are large. Turn several times during cooking, so that all sides are exposed to the heat. When the corn is done, quickly remove the husks or foil and roll the ears around on the grill above the coals for just a minute or two, so that they begin to show spots of browning.

Serve the corn with the remaining seasoned butter on the side.

OKRA AND TOMATO TAGINE

Serves 4

Be sure to choose small okra or ladies' fingers. In North Africa, the okra are threaded on string, so they can be lifted out when the tagine (stew) is stirred. Serve as a main course or with broiled vegetables.

INGREDIENTS

1 lb fresh okra

3 Tbsp olive oil

1 large onion, chopped fine

2 garlic cloves, chopped fine

Pinch of paprika

Pinch of cayenne pepper

1½ lb well-flavored tomatoes, peeled, seeded, and chopped

4 Tbsp chopped fresh parsley

Salt and ground black pepper

Trim the stalks off the okra without cutting the pods. Heat the oil in a pan and fry the okra until lightly browned. Remove with a slotted spoon.

Add the onion and garlic to the pan and fry until soft but not browned. Stir in the paprika and cayenne pepper, stirring for 30 seconds, then add the tomatoes. Bring to a boil and simmer for 10 minutes.

Add the okra, half the parsley, plenty of pepper, and a little salt. Simmer, stirring occasionally, for about 30 minutes.

If the sauce is not well reduced, transfer the okra to a warm dish and keep warm. Boil the sauce until thickened. Pour over the okra. Serve warm or cold, sprinkled with the remaining parsley.

CORN SALSA

Makes about 1¹/₂ cups

Corn salsa is colorful and crunchy, and the jalapeños add gentle heat. For a spicier salsa, don't trim the veins and the seeds from the jalapeños.

INGREDIENTS

1 cup corn kernels	1 Tbsp chopped fresh cilantro
3 Tbsp red bell pepper, diced	2 Tbsp olive oil
3 Tbsp green bell pepper, diced	2 Tbsp fresh lime juice
2 jalapeño chiles, seeded and chopped	¹/₄ tsp ground cumin
1 oz scallions, chopped	¹/₄ tsp salt
1 large tomato, seeded and chopped	Pinch of black pepper

Put the corn kernels in a small saucepan with 3 tablespoons boiling water. Cook until just tender, about 7 minutes. Drain and leave to cool. Meanwhile, combine all the remaining ingredients. Stir in the corn. Let stand for about 15 minutes for the flavors to blend, then taste and adjust the seasoning.

WELL-SEASONED MUSHROOMS

Serves 4–6

This dish is wonderful when made with wild mushrooms, but use cultivated ones if they are not available.

Serve with fried or toasted bread.

INGREDIENTS

1 large onion, chopped fine

4 Tbsp olive oil

2 garlic cloves, chopped fine

½ chile, seeded and chopped, or cayenne pepper to taste

2 lb mushrooms (preferably including

porcini), cleaned and sliced

Salt and ground black pepper

¼ cup dry white wine

2 Tbsp brandy

2 Tbsp chopped fresh parsley

Fry the onion in the oil in a large flameproof casserole, adding the garlic and chile or cayenne pepper once it has softened. Add the sliced mushrooms and fry until they soften. Season and add the wine and brandy. Cook to reduce the liquid a little, sprinkle with parsley, and serve.

SLIGHTLY SPICY LEEKS

Serves 4

The combination of orange, leek, and spice is delicious, however, if the orange clashes with your main dish it may be omitted or the rind of half a lemon may be added instead.

INGREDIENTS

4 Tbsp oil

2 Tbsp crushed coriander seeds

Grated rind and juice of 1 orange

¼ tsp allspice

1 lb leeks, sliced thin and separated into rings

Salt and ground black pepper

Heat the oil, then stir-fry the crushed coriander with the orange rind and allspice over fairly low heat for 2 to 3 minutes, or until the orange rind is quite bright and the mixture is fragrant.

Toss in all the leeks and increase the heat, then stir-fry the vegetables for 8 minutes, or until they are softened. Add the orange juice and boil hard for 2 minutes, tossing the leeks to coat them in a spicy glaze. Taste and season, then serve at once.

SPICY RICE STUFFING WITH GREENS

Serves 4

This rice dish was designed as a stuffing, but you can serve it as a side dish, too.
The almonds add crunch, and the greens add a subtle flavor.

INGREDIENTS

2 cups cleaned and chopped
mustard greens

2–4 Tbsp vegetable oil

1 cup chopped onion

¼ cup chopped celery

½ cup chopped green bell pepper

2 garlic cloves, minced

1 cup vegetable broth

¼ tsp black pepper

¼ tsp salt

¼ tsp cayenne pepper

½ tsp dry mustard

¼ tsp ground cumin

⅓ cup slivered almonds, toasted (see note)

3 cups cooked rice

2 green onions, chopped

Wash the mustard greens at least twice. Run enough water into the sink to cover the greens. Swish the greens through the water, lift them out, and drain the water. Then rinse any sand from the sink, refill with fresh water, and clean again, until all the grit has been washed out. Dry the greens with paper towels or in a salad spinner. Cut out and discard the coarse part of the stem. Chop the greens into 1-inch pieces. In a medium skillet, sauté the greens in 2 tablespoons oil until the greens are limp, 4 to 5 minutes. Remove the greens from the pan and set aside.

Add oil to the pan if needed, and sauté the onion, celery, green bell pepper, and garlic until they are tender, about 5 minutes. Add the vegetable broth and spices. Cook over medium heat until the liquids are slightly reduced. Add the greens, almonds, rice, and green onions. Stir well. Any excess stuffing can be cooked 20 minutes, covered, in a lightly oiled casserole dish.

Note: to toast almonds, spread in a single layer on baking sheet. Bake in 350°F oven until lightly browned, 10 minutes.

SALADS

ASPARAGUS AND MUSHROOM SALAD

Serves 4

The combination of asparagus and mushrooms makes a sophisticated salad. Just be sure that you give the asparagus a head start on the vinaigrette: mushrooms are notorious sponges, and will soak up the dressing before the asparagus has a chance to absorb any of the flavor.

INGREDIENTS

1½ lb fresh asparagus	¼ tsp fresh thyme
2 Tbsp white wine vinegar	¼ tsp fresh oregano or a pinch of dried oregano
½ cup olive oil	
¼ tsp Dijon mustard	¼ tsp salt
1 garlic clove, minced	Pinch of ground black pepper
¼ tsp snipped fresh chives	4 oz mushrooms

Snap the bottoms off the asparagus spears. Blanch 3 to 5 minutes in boiling water, depending on the thickness of the spears. Drain and chill.

Prepare the vinaigrette by mixing all the remaining ingredients except the mushrooms. Shake well and pour over the asparagus.

After the asparagus has been in the vinaigrette for at least 20 minutes, clean, trim, and slice the mushrooms. Add them to the salad, and spoon some of the vinaigrette over them. Allow to marinate for at least another 20 minutes.

MINTED EGGPLANT SALAD WITH YOGURT

Serves 4–6

A creamy salad that can be spiced up a bit with toasted cumin seeds, fennel or coriander seeds.

INGREDIENTS

1 Tbsp cumin seeds

½ cup fruity olive oil

1 large eggplant, sliced

1 garlic clove, minced

2 Tbsp chopped fresh mint

1 cup plain yogurt

Salt and ground black pepper

Heat a large, ridged skillet over moderate heat, then add the cumin seeds and dry roast for 30 seconds, until fragrant and just starting to pop. Transfer to a saucer and leave until required.

Heat the oil in the pan, then add the eggplant slices and fry on both sides until lightly browned and tender. Do not be tempted to add more oil as some will run from the eggplant as it cooks. Remove the slices from the skillet and allow to cool a little, then place them in a shallow dish, sprinkle with the cumin, garlic, and mint and leave until cold.

Spoon on the yogurt and season well. Serve lightly chilled.

SPINACH AND FIG SALAD

Serves 4

A low-calorie salad that looks exotic, yet it is surprisingly quick and simple to make.

INGREDIENTS

1 lb fresh spinach, washed

¼ cup pine nuts

3 fresh figs

Dressing (recipe follows)

A few fresh nasturtium flowers (optional)

For the dressing

⅓ cup olive oil

2 Tbsp fresh lemon juice

Salt and ground black pepper

Remove and discard any coarse stems from the spinach and tear the leaves into pieces. Place in a colander to drain well. Place the pine kernels in a small, dry pan and roast until lightly browned, stirring all the time. Remove from the pan and allow to cool.

Wash the figs, trim off the stems, cut each into quarters and then into thin slices. Place the spinach, pine kernels, and figs into a serving bowl. Make the dressing, and sprinkle over the dressing, toss well, and garnish with a few fresh nasturtium flowers, if available.

CUCUMBER SALAD

Serves 4

You can use cucumbers from the grocery store if you wish, but the ones from your garden will work just as well. This salad benefits from a couple of hours' marinating.

INGREDIENTS

2 large cucumbers, peeled and sliced thin

½ Vidalia or other sweet onion, sliced thin

½ sweet red bell pepper, cut into julienne strips

For the dressing

⅓ cup olive oil

2 Tbsp fresh lemon juice

1 garlic clove, minced

2 tsp minced fresh parsley

1 tsp minced fresh tarragon

¼ tsp salt

Ground black pepper

Put the cucumber, onion, and pepper in a bowl. Make the dressing by combining all the remaining ingredients, then whisk or shake well. Pour the dressing over the salad.

TOMATO SALAD WITH OLIVE SALSA

Serves 4

This simple salad depends on excellent ingredients—perfectly ripe tomatoes, fresh (not prepacked) mozzarella cheese, and fresh basil leaves. Top it with salsa for a luscious summer dish.

INGREDIENTS

4 large, ripe tomatoes

Several sprigs of fresh basil

4 oz fresh mozzarella cheese

About 1 cup salsa mixed with fresh, pitted olives

Core the tomatoes and cut them into thick slices. Arrange the slices on four salad plates. Rinse the basil, pull off the leaves, and dry them between paper towels. Arrange the basil leaves on top of the tomato slices. Cut the mozzarella into thin slices and place on top of the tomato and basil. Spoon the salsa over the tomatoes and cheese.

JICAMA–ORANGE SALAD

Serves 4–6

This refreshing salad combines the crunch of fresh jicama, the tang of oranges, the bite of onion, and the heat of jalapeño chile. It is served with a slightly sweet dressing for an unusual flavor.

INGREDIENTS

3 medium oranges

$1/2$ medium red onion

6 oz peeled jicama, cut into $1/2$-inch cubes

Dressing (recipe follows)

Lettuce leaves

For the dressing

6 Tbsp olive oil

3 Tbsp red wine vinegar

2 Tbsp orange juice

2 tsp honey

$1/4$ tsp chili powder

1 jalapeño chile, unseeded, chopped fine

Peel the oranges and slice them thinly, removing the seeds. Thinly slice the onion, then separate the slices into rings. Mix the orange, onion, and jicama together. Combine all the ingredients in a bottle and shake well to mix.

Toss with the dressing, and serve over lettuce.

Tomato Salad with Olive Salsa ▶

BEAN SPROUT SALAD

Serves 4

A light, crisp salad that makes an excellent appetizer or side dish.

INGREDIENTS

1 lb fresh bean sprouts

1 tsp salt

2½ quarts water

2 Tbsp light soy sauce

1 Tbsp white wine vinegar

2 Tbsp sesame seed oil

2 scallions, shredded fine

Wash and rinse the bean sprouts in cold water discarding the husks and other bits and pieces that float to the surface. It is not necessary to trim each sprout. Blanch the sprouts in a pan of salted, boiling water. Pour them into a colander and rinse in cold water until cool. Drain.

Place the bean sprouts in a bowl or a deep dish and add the soy sauce, vinegar, and sesame seed oil. Toss well and garnish with scallions just before serving.

EGGPLANT, FENNEL, AND WALNUT SALAD

Serves 6

The slightly aniseed flavor of the fennel and the crunch of the nuts contrast well with the eggplant.

INGREDIENTS

¾ cup olive oil

1 fennel bulb, sliced thin, feathery leaves reserved for garnish

1 small red onion, sliced

¾ cup walnut pieces

Sea salt and ground black pepper

1 large eggplant, cut into ½-inch pieces

1 Tbsp red wine vinegar

1 tomato, skinned, seeded and chopped

1 Tbsp torn fresh basil leaves

Fennel leaves and basil sprigs, to garnish

Heat 3 tablespoons of olive oil in a skillet and add the fennel and onion. Cook until just soft but not browned, about 5 to 8 minutes. Remove with a slotted spoon and place in a salad bowl.

Add 2 tablespoons of oil to the skillet, then stir in the walnut pieces and fry them for about 2 minutes, until crisp and browned but not burnt. Remove the nuts from the skillet with a slotted spoon and drain on paper towels. Place the nuts in a bowl, sprinkle with salt, and toss until well coated and cool.

Add 4 tablespoons of oil to the skillet, then add the eggplant and fry over medium heat until tender and browned on all sides. Remove from the pan and add to the fennel and onion. Add the remaining oil to the skillet with the red wine vinegar and a little salt and pepper. Heat, stirring, until the dressing is simmering, then pour over the vegetables in the bowl. Toss lightly, then allow to cool for 10 to 15 minutes.

When the salad is still slightly warm, add the walnuts, chopped tomato, and basil. Leave until cold, then serve garnished with fennel leaves and basil sprigs.

MEDITERRANEAN SALAD

Serves 4

Any combination of vegetables would be delicious steeped in this tomato and garlic sauce.
Be sure to chill the dish well before serving and have crusty bread to hand to mop up the juices.

INGREDIENTS

1¼ cups vegetable broth

1 onion, chopped fine

1 garlic clove, minced

¼ cup dry white wine

4 tomatoes, peeled and chopped

Juice of 1 lime

1 Tbsp cider vinegar

2 tsp tomato paste

1 tsp fennel seeds

1 tsp mustard seeds

1 cup button mushrooms, quartered

2 oz fine beans, trimmed

1 zucchini, sliced

Ground black pepper

Basil sprig, to garnish

Heat the broth in a large saucepan and cook the onion and garlic for 3 to 4 minutes. Add the wine, tomatoes, lime juice, vinegar, tomato paste, fennel, and mustard seeds, and the vegetables. Bring the mixture to a boil, reduce the heat, and simmer for 20 minutes or until the vegetables are just cooked. Season to taste with black pepper.

Transfer the mixture to a serving dish, cover, and chill for at least 1 hour. Garnish with basil and serve.

WARM MUSHROOM SALAD

Serves 4

This is quintessential bistro fare. You could, if you liked, add a handful of shredded prosciutto and/or toasted filberts to this simply prepared but delicious salad.

INGREDIENTS

12 oz small thin asparagus, tough ends broken off	4 oz goat cheese, crumbled or broken into small pieces
3 shallots, chopped	12 oz mixed fresh mushrooms, such as
2 garlic cloves, chopped	oyster, chanterelles, enoki, porcini, and
4 Tbsp olive oil	button, cut into strips or bite-size pieces
7 oz mixed salad greens	1 Tbsp balsamic vinegar
Salt and ground black pepper	12 Tbsp chopped fresh chervil
1 Tbsp tarragon mustard	2 Tbsp snipped fresh chives or chopped
1 tbsp raspberry or red wine vinegar	fresh tarragon

Cook the asparagus in rapidly boiling salted water until just tender and bright green, about 3 minutes. Drain, submerge in very cold water (add a few ice cubes to the water) to keep its bright green color and crisp texture, then drain once again. Set the asparagus aside while you prepare the rest of the salad.

Mix 1 tablespoon of the chopped shallots with half the garlic and 1 to 2 tablespoons olive oil. Toss with the greens, along with salt and pepper to taste. Mix 1 tablespoon olive oil with the tarragon mustard and the raspberry or red wine vinegar; stir well to combine, then pour it over the greens and toss well. Arrange the asparagus and goat cheese over the top.

Sauté the mushrooms over medium-high heat, with the remaining shallots and garlic, in the remaining olive oil until lightly browned. Pour in the balsamic vinegar, season with salt and pepper, then pour this hot mixture over the salad. Serve immediately, with the herbs scattered over the top.

ANDALUCIAN CHOPPED VEGETABLE SALAD

Serves 4

When the weather is hot, make up vats of this stuff and eat it chilled for any meal—even breakfast, when it is exquisitely refreshing. It makes a very nice relish for a bocadillo, a crusty Spanish sandwich.

INGREDIENTS

1 large cucumber, diced	3–5 garlic cloves, minced
3–5 small, ripe tomatoes, diced	¼ tsp ground cumin or cumin seeds
1 carrot, diced	Salt
1 red bell pepper, diced	Juice of 1 lemon
1 green bell pepper, diced	1 tsp sherry vinegar or white wine vinegar
3–5 scallions, sliced thin, or 1 small onion, chopped	3 Tbsp extra virgin olive oil or to taste
	Herbs of your choice

Combine the cucumber, tomatoes, carrot, red and green bell peppers, scallions, and garlic. Toss with cumin, salt, lemon, sherry or white wine vinegar, olive oil, and herbs. Taste for seasoning, and chill until ready to eat.

EGYPTIAN VEGETABLE SALAD

Serves 4

Ful beans, or dried fava beans, are used widely in Egyptian cuisine. They are often simply served drizzled with olive oil with a salad garnish. Here they are used in a salad. Serve accompanied with warmed pita breads.

INGREDIENTS

1½ cups cooked borlotti or fava beans	Large pinch of salt
2–3 hard-cooked eggs, preferably still warm, peeled, and diced	1 onion, chopped
	Handful of arugula, chopped coarse
Extra virgin olive oil, as desired, preferably a North African, Greek, or Turkish oil	2–3 ripe tomatoes, chopped
	1 Tbsp each: cilantro, dill weed, mint
3–4 garlic cloves, minced	2 lemons, cut into wedges

Warm the beans in their juices, then drain, and arrange on a platter. Garnish with the eggs.

Work several tablespoons of the olive oil into the garlic, then pour this over the beans. Season and sprinkle the onion, arugula, tomatoes, cilantro, dill, and mint around the top, and garnish with lemon. Drizzle extra olive oil over the top, and serve with a cruet of olive oil and a bowl of coarse sea salt for sprinkling.

◄ *Andalucian Chopped Vegetable Salad*

FATTOUSH

Serves 4

This salad of stale bread and salad vegetables from Lebanon, characteristically dressed with lots of olive oil and lemon, is very refreshing. A sprinkle of sumac—a tart, red berry related to poison sumac, but not harmful—gives a distinctive tang. Serve it with a helping of yogurt, or yogurt mixed with feta cheese.

INGREDIENTS

1 large or 2 small cucumbers, diced	*3 garlic cloves, chopped*
3 ripe tomatoes, diced	*½ cup extra virgin olive oil*
1 green bell pepper, diced	*Juice of 3 lemons*
8 Tbsp each: fresh mint, cilantro, parsley, chopped	*1 tsp sumac*
3 scallions, sliced thin	*3–4 pita breads, stale and lightly toasted, then broken into pieces*
1 tsp salt	

Combine the cucumbers, tomatoes, bell pepper, mint, cilantro, parsley, scallions, salt, garlic, olive oil, lemon juice, and sumac. Chill for at least 1 hour. Just before serving, toss with the broken pita breads.

BULGAR, RED BELL PEPPER, CUCUMBER, AND CHEESE SALAD

Serves 4–6

Oil-cured black olives can also be added to this salad just before serving, if you like.

INGREDIENTS

1½ cups bulgar wheat

1¼ cups boiling water

4 Tbsp olive oil

3 Tbsp lemon juice

Salt and ground black pepper

3 Tbsp chopped fresh cilantro

2 Tbsp chopped fresh mint

1 red bell pepper, broiled, peeled, and
sliced

1 bunch of plump scallions, chopped

2 garlic cloves, chopped

½ cucumber, chopped coarse

2 cups crumbled feta cheese

Lime wedges and olives, to serve

Place the bulgar wheat in a large bowl, add the boiling water, and leave to soak for 30 minutes, stirring occasionally with a fork, until the water has been absorbed.

In a mixing bowl, whisk together the oil, lemon juice, and seasoning. Pour the oil mixture over the bulgar wheat, add the herbs, and mix well. Then mix in the remaining ingredients. Cover and chill until required. Serve garnished with lime wedges and olives, if you like.

ROASTED PUMPKIN SALAD

Serves 4

Complementary flavors that pack a punch! Serve this salad warm or cold, on a bed of arugula leaves if you wish, with plenty of Italian flat bread to mop up the delicious juices. You could add a few shavings of Parmesan cheese, if you like.

INGREDIENTS

8 slices from a small pumpkin, each about

¾-inch thick, seeded

1 eggplant, quartered lengthwise

2 large slicing tomatoes, halved

6–8 elephant garlic cloves, unpeeled

Salt and ground black pepper

Sugar

Olive oil bread, to serve

6–8 basil leaves, torn in half

For the dressing

6 Tbsp extra virgin olive oil

1 Tbsp balsamic or sherry vinegar

1 tsp Dijon mustard

1 tsp chopped fresh young lovage

leaves or 1 Tbsp chopped fresh

Italian parsley

Salt and ground black pepper

Pinch of sugar

Preheat a 425°F oven. Arrange the prepared vegetables with the garlic in a roasting pan, then season with salt and pepper. Push the basil leaves into the flesh of the tomatoes, then scatter over a little sugar. Drizzle everything with olive oil, then roast at the top of the oven for 40 to 45 minutes, until the vegetables are just starting to blacken. (Check after 30 minutes and remove the tomatoes if they are already soft.)

Allow the vegetables to cool slightly, then cut the pumpkin away from the skin. Leave the vegetables for 10 minutes, if you intend to serve the salad warm, or until completely cold.

Prepare the dressing by blending all the ingredients together and season with salt, pepper, and sugar to taste. Peel the garlic, then arrange the vegetables on four serving plates. Pour the dressing over and add a little fresh basil to each helping. Serve immediately with plenty of olive oil bread.

ROASTED SQUASH, VEGETABLE AND PASTA SALAD

Serves 4

Enjoy this filling salad as a main course or reduce the quantities and serve as an appetizer.

INGREDIENTS

4 x 1-inch slices crown prince squash,
seeded

2 yellow zucchini, trimmed

1 large eggplant, halved lengthwise

1 large red bell pepper

1 garlic bulb

Salt and ground black pepper

Olive oil

7 oz fresh or dried tagliatelle, spaghetti,
or other noodles

Mixed salad leaves, to serve

Salt and ground black pepper

For the dressing

6 Tbsp extra virgin olive oil

2 Tbsp balsamic vinegar

1 tsp Dijon mustard

Sugar

Preheat a 425°F oven. Place all the vegetables in a roasting pan, season lightly, and drizzle with olive oil. Roast for 40 minutes, or until tender and beginning to blacken. Turn the zucchini, bell pepper, and eggplant during cooking, and remove the vegetables as they are done.

Cover the bell peppers with a damp cloth as soon as they come out of the oven, then allow all the vegetables to cool. Peel the skins away from the bell peppers as soon as they are cool enough to handle, then remove their cores and seeds.

Blend all the ingredients for the dressing together. Cook the pasta in plenty of boiling salted water according to the instructions on the package. Drain in a colander and shake briefly, then turn into a serving dish, and add half the vinaigrette. Toss briefly, then allow to cool.

Peel the squash, then chop the roasted vegetables into bite-sized pieces, and squeeze the garlic cloves from their skins. Pile the vegetables over the pasta, then top with the salad leaves. Pour the remaining dressing over the salad, season then toss together just before serving.

SIDE DISHES AND ACCOMPANIMENTS

ORIENTAL BEAN SPROUTS

Serves 4

Bean sprouts are the main ingredient for a chop suey—however, the combination of vegetables may be changed to suit the season or the contents of the salad drawer in the refrigerator.

INGREDIENTS

2 tsp cornstarch

2 Tbsp soy sauce

1 Tbsp dry sherry

2 Tbsp oil

1 tsp sesame seed oil

1 celery stalk, cut into fine short strips

1 green bell pepper, seeded and cut into fine short strips

½ onion, sliced thin

12 oz bean sprouts

Blend the cornstarch with the soy sauce, sherry, and 2 tablespoons of water; set aside.

Heat both oils together, then stir-fry the celery, bell pepper, and onion for 5 minutes. The vegetables should be lightly cooked and still crunchy. Toss in the bean sprouts and stir-fry for 1 minute. Give the cornstarch mixture a stir, pour it into the pan, and bring the juices to a boil, stirring all the time. Cook for 2 minutes, stirring, then serve at once.

GREEN BEANS AND NEW POTATOES IN PESTO

Serves 4

Although this dish takes advantage of the bounty of summer gardens, it can be made with potatoes and green beans that are available year-round, and pesto that is made in quantity during the summer, and frozen in small batches.

INGREDIENTS

1 lb tiny new potatoes, washed and cut in half	²/₃ cup Parmesan or Romano cheese, freshly shredded if possible
1 lb green beans, washed and trimmed	¹/₃ cup olive oil
2 Tbsp pine nuts or chopped walnuts	¹/₄ tsp salt
1 garlic clove, peeled	Pinch of ground black pepper
1 cup loosely packed fresh basil leaves	

Boil the potatoes for 10 minutes. Boil the green beans until tender, 3 to 4 minutes. While the potatoes and beans are cooking, put the remaining ingredients in a food processor and process for 10 seconds, until the basil is chopped but the mixture is not turned into a paste.

Drain the potatoes and beans. Toss with the pesto.

COUSCOUS WITH DRIED APRICOTS AND ALMONDS

Serves 8

INGREDIENTS

12 oz precooked couscous

Scant ¹⁄₂ cup ready-to-eat dried apricots, sliced into strips

Salt and ground black pepper

¹⁄₂ cup blanched almonds, lightly toasted

Chopped fresh cilantro, to serve

Butter or olive oil, to serve (optional)

Put the couscous in a bowl and pour over 2¹⁄₂ cups water. Leave for about 30 minutes or until most of the water has been absorbed; stir frequently with a fork to keep the grains separate. Stir the apricots and seasoning into the couscous then tip into a steamer or metal colander lined with cheesecloth. Place over a saucepan of boiling water, cover tightly with aluminum foil, and steam for about 20 minutes until hot. Stir in the almonds, cilantro, and butter or oil, if using.

TRIO OF PUREES

Serves 4

INGREDIENTS

10 oz potatoes, cubed

1 cup cubed carrots

Grated rind of 1 orange

1 Tbsp orange juice

Ground black pepper

8 oz sweet potato, cubed

Pinch of grated nutmeg

4 oz spinach

Grated rind of 1 lemon

1 Tbsp chopped fresh cilantro

Cook the potatoes in boiling water for 20 minutes until soft. Drain and mash. Divide equally into three separate bowls. Boil the carrots for 10 minutes until soft. Drain and mash. Add to one bowl of potato with the orange rind and juice. Season with pepper.

Cook the sweet potato for 10 minutes in boiling water. Drain and mash. Add to another bowl of potato with the nutmeg. Season with pepper.

Blanch the spinach for 3 minutes in boiling water. Drain very well. Add to the remaining bowl with the lemon rind and cilantro. Season with pepper.

Place the contents of each bowl, separately, in a food processor and blend each for 1 minute each. Spoon one-quarter of the carrot purée into the base of four lightly greased individual ramekin dishes. Top with one-quarter of the spinach mixture and spoon over one-quarter of the sweet potato mixture.

Place the dishes in a roasting pan and fill with enough boiling water to come halfway up the sides. Cover and cook at 375°F for 1 hour. Remove from the roasting pan. Turn out the purées onto serving plates. Serve with a main vegetable dish.

Coucous with Dried Apricots and Almonds ▶

HERBED CAULIFLOWER

Serves 4

Cauliflower cheese traditionally has a rich cheese sauce coating the cauliflower.
This low-fat version uses a wine and herb sauce which is equally delicious.

INGREDIENTS

4 baby cauliflowers	1¼ cups skim milk
2 mint sprigs	⅔ cup dry white wine
3¾ cups vegetable broth	2 Tbsp cornstarch
¼ cup shredded cheese	1 Tbsp chopped fresh parsley
	1 Tbsp chopped fresh cilantro
For the sauce	1 Tbsp chopped fresh thyme
⅔ cup vegetable broth	Ground black pepper

Trim the cauliflowers and place in a large pan with the mint and broth. Cook gently for 10 minutes. Meanwhile, place the broth for the sauce, the milk, and white wine in a pan. Blend the cornstarch with 4 tablespoons of cold water and add to the pan. Bring to a boil, stirring, and add the herbs. Season and simmer for 2 to 3 minutes.

Drain the cauliflower and place in an ovenproof dish. Pour on the sauce and top with the cheese. Broil for 2 to 3 minutes until the cheese has melted. Serve immediately.

MINTED BEANS AND CUCUMBER

Serves 4

Cucumber is not usually served hot, but it is cooked perfectly with the beans in this recipe and delicately flavored with mint. An unusual but delicious side dish.

INGREDIENTS

1 lb fine beans, trimmed

½ cucumber, sliced thick

2 garlic cloves, minced

4 mint sprigs

1 Tbsp lemon juice

⅓ cup vegetable broth

Ground black pepper

Strips of lemon rind, to garnish

Place the vegetables on a large sheet of aluminum foil. Bring up the sides of the foil around the vegetables and crimp to form an open package. Add the remaining ingredients, season, and seal the top of the package.

Place the package in a steamer and cook for 25 minutes or until the beans are tender. Garnish and serve

POTATOES AND SPINACH

Serves 4

This is one of the most popular Bhajis, especially if a bunch of fresh fenugreek leaves is added to it. These leaves are called methi *and can be obtained from most Asian grocers all year round. If you find some use the leaves only and substitute these for 2 oz of the spinach.*

INGREDIENTS

14 oz fresh or frozen leaf spinach	2¹⁄₂ oz tomato, chopped
8 oz potatoes	¹⁄₄ tsp turmeric
2 Tbsp oil	¹⁄₂ tsp chili powder
¹⁄₄ tsp fenugreek seeds	Salt to taste
¹⁄₂ tsp cumin seeds	

If you are using fresh spinach, weigh it after you have removed the stalks and chopped it. Wash it thoroughly to remove all the hidden grit and leave it to drain in a colander. If you are using frozen spinach, defrost it and let it drain well in a colander.

Scrub the potatoes well and do not peel them. Cut the potatoes into quarters, then cut each quarter into 2 or more pieces, making 8 to 12 pieces from each potato. Heat the oil in a medium-sized heavy pan and fry the fenugreek and cumin seeds. As the seeds begin to sizzle, add the tomato, turmeric, chili powder, and salt. Mix and cook the mixture for half a minute. Add the spinach and potato, and mix thoroughly so that the vegetables become well coated in the spices.

Cover the pan and simmer for 15 to 20 minutes. If there is still a little moisture left after this time, remove the lid and dry it out a little by cooking rapidly over medium to high heat for another few minutes, taking care not to let it burn.

PUMPKIN WITH LEEKS

Serves 4

Stir-frying is one of the best cooking methods for pumpkin—the vegetable remains whole but slightly tender.

INGREDIENTS

2 Tbsp oil

Knob of butter

1 garlic clove, minced

2 leeks, sliced

2 tsp ground cinnamon

2 oz sultanas

1 lb pumpkin flesh, seeded and cubed

Salt and ground black pepper

Heat the oil and butter until the butter melts, then add the garlic, leeks, cinnamon, and sultanas. Stir-fry the leeks for 5 minutes until they are softened and tender.

Add the pumpkin and seasoning. Continue stir-frying until the cubes are tender, but not soft enough to become mushy, which takes about 7 to 10 minutes. Serve the dish at once.

SWEET RED CABBAGE

Serves 4

Colorful and with a sweet and sour flavor, this dish may also be served cold.

INGREDIENTS

1¼ cups vegetable broth

1½ lb red cabbage, cored and shredded

1 onion, sliced

1 Tbsp granulated brown sugar

1 tsp ground allspice

8 oz green apples, cored and sliced

1 tsp fennel seeds

2 Tbsp cider vinegar

1 Tbsp cornstarch

1 Tbsp chopped fresh parsley

Place half of the broth in a large saucepan. Add the cabbage and onion and cook over high heat for 5 minutes. Add the sugar, allspice, apples, fennel seeds, vinegar, and remaining broth. Blend the cornstarch with 2 tablespoons of cold water to form a paste. Stir into the pan and bring to a boil, stirring until thickened and clear.

Reduce the heat and cook for 15 minutes more until the cabbage is cooked. Sprinkle with the parsley and serve the dish immediately.

CARAMELIZED BAKED ONIONS

Serves 4

These baked onions have a slightly "burnt" taste which complements the sweetness of the onion. Serve with a simple main dish.

INGREDIENTS

4 large onions

2 tsp polyunsaturated margarine

5 Tbsp granulated brown sugar

Cut the onions into quarters and then into four again. Cook in boiling water for 10 minutes. Drain well.

Place the margarine and sugar in a pan and heat gently until melted.

Place the onions in a roasting pan and pour over the margarine and sugar. Cook in the oven at 375°F for 10 minutes until browned. Serve immediately.

Sweet Red Cabbage ▶

THREE-MUSHROOM FRY

Serves 4

This really is a simple yet delicious dish. Three varieties of mushroom are cooked in garlic and soy sauce.

INGREDIENTS

3 oz open cap mushrooms

3 oz oyster mushrooms

3 oz shiitake mushrooms

4 Tbsp vegetable broth

2 garlic cloves, minced

1 Tbsp soy sauce

2 Tbsp chopped fresh parsley or thyme

Ground black pepper

Peel the open cap mushrooms and slice thinly. Place all the mushrooms in a skillet with the broth, garlic, soy sauce, and half of the herbs. Season well with black pepper. Cook, stirring, for 3 to 4 minutes. Sprinkle in the remaining herbs and serve immediately.

CAULIFLOWER AND POTATO CURRY

Serves 2–3

A classic Indian side dish.

INGREDIENTS

6 Tbsp oil

1 lb potatoes, peeled and quartered

1 small cauliflower, cut into large florets

Pinch of asafoetida

$^{3}/_{4}$ tsp ground turmeric

$^{1}/_{2}$ tsp chili powder

$1^{1}/_{2}$ tsp ground cumin

$^{3}/_{4}$ tsp salt

Large pinch of sugar

2 tomatoes, chopped

2 tsp ghee

$^{1}/_{2}$ tsp garam masala

Heat the oil in a large pan or wok over medium high heat. Fry the potatoes a few pieces at a time until slightly brown. Remove and set aside. Fry the cauliflower pieces a few at a time until brown spots appear on them. Remove and set aside.

Lower the heat to medium, add the asafoetida, and after 3 to 4 seconds, add the turmeric, chili, cumin, salt, and sugar.

Mix the spices together, add the tomatoes, and fry for 1 minute with the spices. Add $1^{1}/_{2}$ **cups** of water and bring to a boil. Put in the potatoes, cover, and cook for 10 minutes. Add the cauliflower, cover again, and cook for a further 5 to 7 minutes until the potatoes and cauliflower are tender. Add the ghee and sprinkle with the garam masala. Remove from the heat and serve hot with rice and red lentils.

◀ *Three-Mushroom Fry*

BEET WITH HORSERADISH

Serves 4

This flavorful side dish could also be served with blinis (Russian pancakes).

INGREDIENTS

4 Tbsp oil

2 onions, halved and sliced thin

1 lb cooked beet, cut in small cubes

Salt and ground black pepper

3 Tbsp chopped fresh dill weed

4 Tbsp horseradish sauce

$\frac{1}{2}$ cup sour cream

Heat the oil and stir-fry the onions for 10 minutes, until they are quite well cooked and beginning to brown. Add the beet with seasoning and continue to stir-fry for about 5 minutes for the beet to become hot, and for the flavor of the onions to mingle with it. Stir in the dill weed and transfer to a serving dish.

Mix the horseradish sauce with the sour cream and trickle this over the beet. Serve at once, tossing the horseradish cream with the beet and onion as the vegetables are spooned out.

CORIANDER POTATOES

Serves 4

Coriander works wonders for new potatoes, complementing their sweet fresh flavor perfectly.

INGREDIENTS

2 lb small new potatoes, scrubbed and boiled

Salt and ground black pepper

2 tsp superfine sugar

2 Tbsp lemon juice

4 Tbsp olive oil

3 Tbsp crushed coriander seeds

Strip of lemon

4 Tbsp snipped chives

Cook the potatoes in boiling, slightly salted water for 10 to 15 minutes, or until tender. Drain. Stir the sugar and lemon juice together until the sugar dissolves completely.

Heat the oil and stir-fry the coriander for 2 minutes. Add the lemon rind and continue to cook for a further minute, pressing the piece of rind to bring out its flavor. Tip the potatoes into the pan and then stir-fry them for about 10 minutes, or until they are just beginning to brown on the outside.

Pour the sweetened lemon juice over the potatoes and mix them well with the oil in the pan, so that the liquids mingle to form a hot dressing. Mix in the chives, check the seasoning, and serve at once.

MIXED VEGETABLE BHAJI

Serves 4

This mixture of vegetables has a new taste every time it is cooked, as the balance of ingredients seems to change.

INGREDIENTS

4 oz green beans	4 oz tomatoes	½ tsp chili powder
6 oz potatoes	1–2 green chiles	¼ tsp turmeric powder
4 oz carrots	2 Tbsp oil	½–¾ tsp salt
6 oz eggplant	7–8 garlic cloves, chopped fine	2–3 Tbsp mint or cilantro leaves

Top and tail and de-string the beans, then chop them into bite-sized lengths. Cut the potatoes into quarters and halve them again, preferably leaving the skin on. Scrape and dice the carrots. Cut the eggplant into 4 strips lengthwise and then slice across into ½-inch chunks. Chop the tomatoes and green chiles.

Measure the oil into a heavy pan over medium heat. Add the garlic, stirring it as soon as it begins to turn translucent, then add all the vegetables. Also stir in the chili powder, turmeric, and salt. Mix the spices together. Lower the heat, cover the pan, and cook for 20 to 25 minutes.

Add the mint or cilantro leaves, stir, and switch the heat off. Let it stand for 2 to 3 minutes before serving.

HOT SPICY LENTILS

Serves 4

Red lentils provide the basis for a substantial side dish which is highly flavored with spices and red chile.

INGREDIENTS

¾ cup red lentils	¼ tsp ground coriander
4 tsp polyunsaturated oil	1 red chile, chopped
1 red onion, chopped	3¾ cups vegetable broth
2 garlic cloves, minced	Juice and grated rind of 1 lime
¼ tsp ground cumin	Ground black pepper

Wash the lentils in 2 to 3 changes of water. Drain and reserve. Heat the oil in a pan, add the onion, garlic, and spices and cook for 5 minutes. Stir in the lentils and cook for 3 to 4 minutes more.

Add the chile and broth, and bring to a boil. Reduce the heat and simmer gently for 35 minutes until the lentils are soft. Stir in the lime juice and rind. Season well and serve.

◀ *Mixed Vegetable Bhaji*

DELICIOUS DESSERTS

HONEYED ORANGES

Serves 4

*Oranges and ginger make a great combination. Ground ginger has been added to
this recipe with a dash of orange liqueur for extra flavor.*

INGREDIENTS

4 Tbsp honey

$\frac{1}{2}$ tsp ground cinnamon

$\frac{1}{4}$ tsp ground ginger

2 mint sprigs

2 tsp Grand Marnier

4 oranges

Place the honey, cinnamon, ginger, and mint in a pan with $\frac{2}{3}$ cup water. Heat gently to melt the honey. Bring to a boil and boil for 3 minutes to reduce by half. Remove the mint from the pan and discard. Stir in the Grand Marnier liqueur.

Meanwhile, peel the oranges, remove the pith, and slice thin. Place the orange slices in a serving bowl, pour over the syrup, and chill for 1 hour before serving.

STRAWBERRY FOOL

Serves 4

*This dish is simple to prepare, but should be made in advance of a meal as it
requires chilling for 1 hour before serving.*

INGREDIENTS

10 oz strawberries, hulled and chopped

$\frac{1}{2}$ cup confectioners' sugar

$1\frac{1}{4}$ cups low-fat plain yogurt

2 egg whites

Strawberry slices and mint sprigs,
to decorate

Place the chopped strawberries in a food processor with the confectioners' sugar. Blend for 30 seconds until smooth. Place the yogurt in a bowl and stir in the strawberry mixture. Whisk the egg whites until peaks form and fold in gently. Spoon into serving glasses and chill for 1 hour. Decorate and serve.

Honeyed Oranges ▶

MELON ICE

Serves 4

*Any melon is suitable for this recipe. Incredibly colorful and refreshing,
it is the perfect light end to any meal.*

INGREDIENTS

½ cup sugar

3 mint sprigs

1 lb melon, such as cantaloupe, galia, or
watermelon, seeded and diced

Mint, to decorate

Set the freezer to rapid freeze. Place the sugar in a pan with ½ cup water. Add the mint and cook over gentle heat until the sugar dissolves. Remove the pan from the heat and strain the syrup. Discard the mint sprigs. Stir in 1¼ cups of cold water.

Place the melon in a food processor and purée for 30 seconds until smooth. Stir into the syrup. Mix well and cool.

Place the mixture in a freezerproof container and freeze for 1 hour.

Remove from the freezer, pour the melon mixture into a bowl, and whisk until smooth. Return to a clean freezerproof container and freeze for a further 30 minutes. Repeat the whisking process every 30 minutes for 2½ hours. Scoop into dishes, decorate with mint, and serve immediately.

APRICOT SHERBET

Serves 4

*Traditionally sherbets are served part way through a meal to clear the palate,
but they are equally welcome at the end.*

INGREDIENTS

¾ cup sugar

Juice of ½ orange

1 lb apricots, pitted and chopped

1 egg white

2 Tbsp fine granulated sugar

Apricot slices, mint sprigs, and orange
rind, to decorate

Set the freezer to rapid freeze. Place the sugar and orange juice in a pan with ⅔ cup water. Cook over gentle heat to dissolve. Add a further 1¼ cups water to the pan. Place the apricots in a food processor and purée for 30 seconds until smooth. Stir the apricot purée into the sugar syrup, place in a freezerproof container, and freeze for 1 hour until half frozen. Whisk the egg white in a clean bowl until peaking and whisk in the sugar.

Turn the half-frozen fruit mixture into a bowl and whisk until smooth. Fold in the egg white and return to a freezerproof container. Freeze for 45 minutes. Turn the mixture out into a bowl, whisk again, and return to a clean freezerproof container. Freeze for a further 2 hours until solid. Place the sherbet in the refrigerator 10 minutes before serving. Scoop into serving dishes, decorate, and serve.

Melon Ice ▶

VANILLA MOUSSE

Serves 4

This light and fluffy mousse tastes as good as it looks. It is sliced and served with a delicious raspberry sauce.

INGREDIENTS

For the mousse

1¼ cups low-fat plain yogurt

⅔ cup skim milk cheese or

cream cheese

1 tsp vanilla extract

4 Tbsp vanilla sugar

1 Tbsp brandy or sherry

2 tsp vegetarian gelatin

2 large egg whites

For the sauce

1¾ cups raspberries

Juice of 1 orange

¼ cup confectioners' sugar, sifted

Place the yogurt, cheese, vanilla extract, sugar, and alcohol in a food processor, blend for 30 seconds until smooth. Pour into a mixing bowl.

Sprinkle the vegetarian gelatin onto 4 tablespoons of cold water in the saucepan. Stir until dissolved and heat to boiling point. Boil for 2 minutes.

Cool, then stir into the yogurt mixture. Whisk the egg whites until peaking and fold into the mousse.

Line a 3¾-cup loaf pan with plastic wrap. Pour the mousse into the prepared pan and chill for 2 hours until set. Meanwhile, place the sauce ingredients in a food processor and blend until smooth. Press through a strainer to discard the seeds. Unmold the mousse onto a plate, remove the wrap, pour a little sauce onto a plate, slice the mousse, and serve.

BANANA ICE CREAM

Serves 4

This is really a cheat ice cream. Made with frozen bananas and plain yogurt, the freezing time of the completed recipe is greatly reduced.

INGREDIENTS

8 oz bananas, chopped and frozen

1 Tbsp lemon juice

6 Tbsp confectioners' sugar

⅔ cup low-fat plain yogurt

Grated rind of 1 lemon

Small meringues, to serve (optional)

Set the freezer to rapid freeze. Place the frozen bananas in a food processor with the lemon juice, sugar, and yogurt. Process for 1 minute or until smooth. Stir in the lemon rind.

Place the mixture in a freezerproof container, cover, and freeze for 2 hours or until set. Scoop into dishes and serve with small meringues, if liked.

◀ *Vanilla Mousse*

BLUEBERRY CHEESECAKE

Serves 6

A cheesecake with a delicious granola and dried fig base.

INGREDIENTS

For the base	For the filling	For the topping
1 cup natural granola	1 tsp vegetarian gelatin	2 cups blueberries
5 oz dried figs	½ cup skim evaporated milk	2 nectarines, pitted and sliced
	1 egg	2 Tbsp clear honey
	6 Tbsp fine granulated sugar	
	2 cups low-fat cottage cheese	
	½ cup blueberries	

Place the granola and dried figs in a food processor and blend together for 30 seconds. Press into the base of a base-lined 8-inch springform pan and chill while preparing the filling.

In a saucepan, sprinkle the gelatin onto 4 tablespoons of cold water. Stir until dissolved and heat to boiling point. Boil for 2 minutes, then cool.

Place the milk, egg, sugar, and cheese in a food processor and blend until smooth. Stir in the blueberries. Place in a mixing bowl and gradually stir in the dissolved gelatin. Pour the mixture onto the base and chill for 2 hours until set.

Remove the cheesecake from the pan and arrange the fruit for the topping in alternate rings on top. Drizzle the honey over the fruit and serve.

CREME CARAMEL
Makes 4

INGREDIENTS

½ cup plus 2 tsp fine granulated sugar
2 eggs, beaten
1¼ cups skim milk
½ tsp vanilla extract
Pinch of ground cinnamon

Dissolve the ½ cup sugar in a pan with ⅔ cup cold water. Bring to a boil and boil rapidly until the mixture begins to turn golden brown. Pour into the base of four x ⅔-cup ramekin dishes.

Whisk the remaining sugar with the eggs in a bowl. Heat the milk with the vanilla and cinnamon until just boiling and gradually whisk into the egg mixture.

Pour into the ramekins and place in a shallow roasting pan with enough hot water to reach halfway up the sides. Cover and cook in the oven at 350°F for 50 minutes until set. Remove from the pan, cool slightly, and chill in the refrigerator for 1 hour. Unmold onto individual plates and serve immediately.

Blueberry Cheesecake ▶

PLUM AND GINGER BRULEE

Serves 4

Plums and ginger are a great combination in this easy brûlée recipe, the ginger adding just enough spice to complement the plums.

INGREDIENTS

4 plums, pitted and chopped

Scant 1 cup half-fat cream

Scant 1 cup low-fat plain yogurt

$^1/_2$ tsp ground ginger

4 Tbsp granulated brown sugar

Spoon the plums into the base of four x $^2/_3$-cup ramekin dishes. Lightly whip the cream and fold in the yogurt and ground ginger. Spoon onto the fruit and chill for 2 hours.

Sprinkle the brown sugar on top of the yogurt mixture and broil for 5 minutes or until the sugar has dissolved. Chill for 20 minutes before serving. Serve garnished with a sprig of mint, if you like.

CAPPUCCINO SPONGES

Serves 4

These individual sponge puddings are delicious served with coffee sauce. Ideal for dinner parties, they look more delicate and attractive than one large pudding.

INGREDIENTS

2 Tbsp polyunsaturated margarine

2 Tbsp granulated brown sugar

2 egg whites

$^1/_2$ cup all-purpose flour

$^3/_4$ tsp baking powder

6 Tbsp skim milk

1 tsp coffee extract

$^1/_2$ tsp unsweetened cocoa powder

For the coffee sauce

$1^1/_4$ cups skim milk

1 Tbsp granulated brown sugar

1 tsp coffee extract

1 tsp coffee liqueur (optional)

2 Tbsp cornstarch

Lightly grease four x $^2/_3$-cup individual pudding molds. Cream the margarine and the sugar together in a bowl and add the egg whites. Sift the flour and baking powder together and fold into the creamed mixture with a metal spoon. Gradually stir in the milk, coffee extract, and cocoa.

Spoon equal amounts of the mixture into the molds. Cover with pleated wax paper, then foil, and tie securely with string. Place in a steamer or pan with sufficient boiling water to reach halfway up the sides of the molds. Cover and cook for 30 minutes or until cooked through.

Meanwhile, place the milk, sugar, coffee extract, and coffee liqueur, if using, in a pan to make the sauce. Blend the cornstarch with 4 tablespoons of cold water and stir into the pan. Bring to a boil, stirring until thickened. Reduce the heat and cook for a further 2 to 3 minutes.

Carefully remove the cooked puddings from the steamer. Remove the paper and foil and unmold onto individual plates. Spoon the sauce around and serve.

Plum and Ginger Brûlée ▶

FIG AND PEACH SOUFFLE

Serves 4

This is a delicious, delicately flavored soufflé. The figs need to be ripe for the best results and the peaches not too large. Lime juice is the preferred choice, but a lemon is a suitable substitute.

INGREDIENTS

8 oz ripe figs	2 Tbsp lime or lemon juice
2 peaches	$\frac{2}{3}$ cup whipping cream, lightly whipped
$\frac{1}{2}$ cup plus 2 Tbsp sugar	
$\frac{1}{4}$ cup water	**To decorate**
3 eggs, separated	Cream, for piping
1 Tbsp vegetarian gelatin dissolved in	1 fig
5 Tbsp hot water	Frosted geranium leaves (if available)

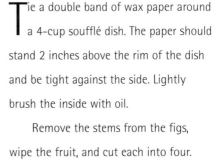

Tie a double band of wax paper around a 4-cup soufflé dish. The paper should stand 2 inches above the rim of the dish and be tight against the side. Lightly brush the inside with oil.

Remove the stems from the figs, wipe the fruit, and cut each into four. Skin the peaches, remove the pits, and cut into four. In a pan, dissolve $\frac{1}{2}$ cup sugar in the water, and put the fruit into the pan and cook very gently to just soften the fruit. Remove, cool, and blend.

Place the egg yolks in a bowl with the remaining 2 tablespoons sugar over a pan of hot water and beat until light and fluffy. Remove the pan from the heat and continue beating until cool. Add the gelatin to the lime or lemon juice and fruit purée, and add this to the egg mixture with the whipped cream. Whisk the egg whites until stiff, fold into the fruit mixture, and pour into the prepared soufflé dish. Put into a cool place until set.

Carefully remove the collar from the soufflé. Pipe cream, optional, around the top edge and decorate with thin slices of figs and geranium leaves (if available).

ICED BLACK CURRANT SOUFFLÉ

Serves 6

Fresh black currants are available June through August. Always select plump juicy fruit.

INGREDIENTS

3 cups black currants, hulled

³/₄ cup sugar

2 egg whites

¹/₂ cup confectioners' sugar, sifted

1¹/₄ cups whipping cream

Wrap a double thickness of aluminum foil around a 4-cup soufflé dish to extend 2 inches above the rim of the dish. Cook the black currants with the sugar until soft, purée in a blender, and then strain. Allow to cool. Whisk the egg whites until stiff, then gradually whisk in the confectioners' sugar.

Whip the cream until softly stiff. Place the fruit purée in a large bowl and gradually fold in the egg white and cream. Pour into the prepared soufflé dish, level the surface, and freeze for several hours until solid. Remove the foil and serve.

SURPRISE BANANA PUFFS

Makes approximately 20 puffs

A delicious fruit-filled variation on profiteroles.

INGREDIENTS

1 lb ripe bananas

Juice of 1 orange

⅓ cup soft brown sugar

1 cup Greek yogurt

For the choux pastry

¼ cup butter or margarine

½ cup water

½ cup plus 2 Tbsp flour

2 eggs

For the caramel sauce

1 cup sugar

8 Tbsp water

Peel and mash the bananas in a bowl with the orange juice and sugar. Whisk in the yogurt, pour into a suitable container and freeze, beating three times at regular intervals.

Place the butter or margarine in a medium-sized saucepan and pour in the water. Heat gently until the fat melts, then turn the heat up and bring to a full boil. Tip in all the flour, remove the pan from the heat, and mix until smooth, when the mixture should come away from the sides of the pan. Allow to cool.

Preheat a 425°F oven. Grease two baking sheets. Have ready a large pastry bag fitted with a large fluted tip.

Beat the eggs and gradually beat into the lukewarm mixture in the pan. Continue beating until the mixture is smooth and glossy. Fill the pastry bag with the mixture and pipe small mounds onto the greased baking sheets, leaving enough space between for the puffs to expand. Bake for 10 minutes, then reduce the oven temperature to 375°F and cook for 10 minutes more. Remove from the oven. Slit and cool on a wire rack.

Make the caramel by placing the sugar and 8 tablespoons of water in a saucepan. Heat gently to dissolve the sugar. When dissolved, bring to a boil and cook until it begins to change color. When the syrup becomes a golden color, cover your hand with a dish cloth, lift the pan from the heat, and quickly dip the base in cold water to stop the caramel overcooking. Add a little boiling water to the pan for a runny caramel for pouring over the puffs. Keep on one side.

Place the ice cream in the refrigerator for 30 minutes before filling the puffs. Serve with the caramel sauce.

GRAPE CUSTARDS

Serves 4

This delightful dessert is so quick and simple to make. It is ideal for a dinner party.

INGREDIENTS

8 oz seedless red grapes

4 egg yolks

3 Tbsp superfine sugar

4 Tbsp Marsala, Madeira or sweet sherry

Wash the grapes and place in the bottom of four individual glasses.

Place the egg yolks in a bowl. Beat lightly, add the sugar and wine, and mix together. Place the bowl over a pan of hot water and whisk until the mixture is thick and creamy. This could take about 10 minutes.

Divide the mixture among the glasses and serve at once while still warm with lady fingers.

ORANGE AND STRAWBERRY SYLLABUB

Serves 6

A tasty fruit version of a syllabub. The fruits may be varied, depending on the time of year.

INGREDIENTS

1¼ cups fresh strawberries

Juice and coarsely grated peel of 1 orange

1 Tbsp Grand Marnier or Cointreau

3 Tbsp superfine sugar

⅔ cup white wine

1 tsp lemon juice

1¼ cups heavy cream

2 egg whites

Wash and hull the strawberries. Slice and arrange in the bottom of six sundae glasses. Sprinkle the orange juice and the liqueur over the top.

Place the superfine sugar, wine, and lemon juice in a mixing bowl. Add half the grated orange peel together with the cream and stir until the ingredients are absorbed by the cream.

Whisk the egg whites until stiff. Add to the cream and continue whisking until the mixture is softly stiff. Spoon on top of the strawberries and sprinkle with the remaining orange peel. Serve well chilled.

GOLDEN SUMMER PUDDING

Serves 6

This is a variation on the theme of the traditional summer pudding.

INGREDIENTS

2 oranges

2 cups water

6 Tbsp granulated sugar

2 peaches or nectarines

2 mangoes

12 slices white bread

To decorate

Slices of mango (optional)

Slices of orange (optional)

Remove the peel from the oranges and place the peel in a saucepan with the water and sugar. Dissolve the sugar and cook gently for 2 minutes to extract the flavor from the orange peel. Remove the pan from the heat and discard the orange peel.

Skin the peaches or nectarines and mangoes, and remove the pits. Cut the flesh into small dice, add to the flavored syrup, and cook to just soften the fruit, about 5 minutes. Remove from the heat.

Cut 12 rounds of bread to fit the base and tops of six ²/₃-cup ramekin dishes and place a round in the base of each dish. Cut small squares of bread and use to line the sides of the dishes.

Using a slotted spoon, fill each dish with the fruit, reserving the syrup to serve with the puddings. Top each with the remaining circles of bread, pressing down well. Cover each tightly with plastic wrap and leave to chill overnight.

To serve, remove carefully from the dishes, spoon the remaining syrup over, and decorate, if liked, with extra slices of mango or orange.

CAKES, BAKES, AND COOKIES

RAISIN AND HONEY BREAD

Serves 16

This loaf contains a high proportion of yogurt which gives it a white, light center.
Serve with butter and preserves for a tasty afternoon treat.

INGREDIENTS

2¼ cups flour

1½ tsp baking powder

½ tsp baking soda

½ tsp salt

1¾ cups low-fat plain yogurt

2 egg whites

⅓ cup raisins

2 Tbsp clear honey

Polyunsaturated margarine, for greasing

Mix the flour, baking powder, baking soda, and salt in a large bowl. Whisk together the yogurt and egg whites, and fold into the flour mixture with the raisins and honey.

Grease a 2-pound loaf pan and spoon in the mixture. Bake in the oven at 425°F for 20 minutes until golden. Cool slightly and turn out of the pan. Serve warm.

OAT AND ORANGE COOKIES

Makes 20

These little cookies are hard to resist. Rolled in oatmeal, they have a crunchy outside, and softer inside which has a mild orange flavor.

INGREDIENTS

3 Tbsp polyunsaturated margarine

¼ cup granulated brown sugar

1 egg white, lightly beaten

2 Tbsp skim milk

3 Tbsp raisins

Grated rind of 1 orange

1¼ cups self-rising flour

⅓ cup oatmeal

Strips of orange rind, to decorate
(optional)

Cream the margarine and sugar together until light and fluffy. Add the egg white, milk, raisins, and orange rind. Fold in the flour and bring the mixture together to form a dough. Roll into 20 equal-sized balls.

Place the oatmeal in a shallow bowl, roll each dough ball in the oatmeal to coat completely, pressing them on gently. Place the cookies on nonstick baking sheets, spacing well apart. Flatten each round slightly.

Bake in the oven at 350°F for 15 minutes or until golden. Cool on a wire rack, decorate, and store any leftovers in an airtight container.

GINGERBREAD

Makes 16 portions

INGREDIENTS

4 cups all-purpose flour

Pinch of salt

1 Tbsp ground ginger

1 Tbsp baking powder

1 tsp baking soda

1 cup granulated brown sugar

½ cup molasses

½ cup corn syrup

⅔ cup dried pitted prunes

1¼ cups skim milk

1 egg white

Powdered confectioners' sugar for dusting

2 pieces preserved ginger, chopped

Grease and line a 9-inch square pan. Sift the flour, salt, ground ginger, baking powder, and baking soda into a large bowl.

Place the sugar, molasses, and syrup in a pan and heat gently to dissolve. Place the dried prunes in a food processor with 3 tablespoons of water and blend for 30 seconds until puréed. Add the milk to the sugar mixture and stir into the dry ingredients with the prunes, mixing well. Whisk the egg white until peaking, fold into the mixture, and spoon into the prepared pan.

Bake in the oven at 325°F for 55 minutes or until firm. Cool in the pan for 10 minutes. Turn the cake out onto a wire rack and cool completely. Cut into 16 pieces. Dust with confectioners' sugar and top with chopped ginger.

CHOCOLATE BROWNIES

Makes 16

These chocolate brownies are low fat – they taste just as good as the real thing but have a slightly different texture. Keep in an airtight container if you can resist them for long enough.

INGREDIENTS

⅔ cup pitted dried prunes

¾ cup granulated brown sugar

3 Tbsp unsweetened cocoa powder, sifted

½ cup all-purpose flour

1 tsp baking powder

3 egg whites

Confectioners' sugar, for dusting

Lightly grease and line a shallow 7-inch square cake pan.

Place the prunes in a food processor with 3 tablespoons of water and blend to a purée. Transfer the purée to a mixing bowl and stir in the sugar, cocoa, flour, and baking powder. Whisk the egg whites until peaking and fold into the mixture. Pour into the prepared pan and level the surface.

Bake in the oven at 350°F for 1 hour or until cooked through. Let the brownies cool in the pan for 10 minutes, then turn out onto a wire rack, and cool completely. Cut into squares, dust with confectioners' sugar, and serve.

Gingerbread ▶

PEAR UPSIDE-DOWN CAKE

Makes 8 slices

In this recipe, sliced pears are set on a caramel base and topped with a spicy sponge mixture. Once cooked, turn out, and serve immediately with plain yogurt.

INGREDIENTS

2 Tbsp clear honey

2 Tbsp granulated brown sugar

2 large pears, peeled, cored, and sliced

4 Tbsp polyunsaturated margarine

1/4 cup fine granulated sugar

3 egg whites

1 cup self-rising flour

2 tsp ground allspice

Heat the honey and sugar in a pan until melted. Pour into a base-lined 8-inch round cake pan. Arrange the pears around the base of the pan.

Cream the margarine and sugar together until light and fluffy. Whisk the egg whites until peaking and fold into the mixture with the flour and allspice. Spoon on top of the pears.

Bake in the oven at 350°F for 50 minutes or until risen. Let sit for 5 minutes, then turn out onto a serving plate. Remove the lining paper, decorate with walnuts (optional), and serve.

FRUIT AND NUT LOAF

Makes 12 slices

This is a sweet fruity bread as opposed to a "tea" bread. If liked, spread slices of the bread with a little butter to serve.

INGREDIENTS

2 cups white bread flour

1/2 tsp salt

1 Tbsp polyunsaturated margarine

1 Tbsp fine granulated sugar

2/3 cup raisins

1/4 cup walnuts, chopped

2 tsp active dry yeast

5 Tbsp skim milk

1 Tbsp clear honey

Sift the flour and salt into a bowl. Rub in the margarine, then stir in the sugar, raisins, walnuts, and yeast. Pour the milk in a pan with 5 tablespoons of water. Heat gently until lukewarm, but do not boil. Add the lukewarm liquid to the dry ingredients in the bowl and bring the mixture together to form a dough.

Turn the dough onto a lightly floured surface and knead the dough for 5 to 7 minutes until smooth and elastic. Shape the dough into a round and place on a nonstick baking sheet. Make parallel diagonal slits across the top of the loaf, working from left to right. Then turn the knife and work back toward you making parallel diagonal slits to form "diamond" shapes. Cover and allow to rise in a warm place for 1 hour or until doubled in size.

Bake in the oven at 425°F for 35 minutes or until cooked through. Place on a wire rack and brush with honey. Cool and serve.

Pear Upside-Down Cake ▶

APPLE BRAN CAKE

Makes 12 slices

*Chunks of apple add moisture to this filling cake. Decorate with apple slices just
before serving or brush with a little lemon juice if you wish to store the cake.*

INGREDIENTS

1/2 cup plus 2 Tbsp apple sauce

1/2 cup plus 2 Tbsp brown sugar

3 Tbsp skim milk

1 1/2 cups all-purpose flour

1 oz all bran cereal

2 tsp baking powder

1 tsp ground cinnamon

2 Tbsp clear honey

5 oz apples, peeled and chopped

2 egg whites

Apple slices and 1 Tbsp honey, to decorate

Lightly grease and base line a deep 8-inch round cake pan.

Place the apple sauce in a mixing bowl with the sugar and milk. Sift the flour into the bowl and add the bran, baking powder, cinnamon, honey, and apples. Whisk the egg whites until peaking and fold into the mixture. Spoon the mixture into the prepared pan and level the surface.

Bake in the oven at 150°F for 1 1/4–1 1/2 hours or until cooked through. Cool in the pan for 10 minutes, then turn onto a wire rack and cool completely. Arrange the apple slices on top and drizzle with honey.

Apple Bran Cake ▶

SEED BREAD

Serves 12

INGREDIENTS

1 package active dry yeast

4 cups whole wheat flour

2 tsp fine granulated sugar

2 tsp salt

2 Tbsp polyunsaturated margarine

2 tsp caraway seeds

2 tsp fennel seeds

2 tsp sesame seeds

1 egg white

Place the yeast, flour, sugar, and salt in a bowl. Rub in the margarine and add half of each of the seeds. Stir in 1¼ cups luke warm water and mix well. Bring the mixture together to form a soft dough. Knead the dough for 5 minutes on a floured surface and break into six pieces.

Lightly grease a deep 6-inch round cake pan. Shape each of the dough pieces into a round. Place five pieces around the edge of the pan and one in the center.

Cover and leave to prove in a warm place for 1 hour or until doubled in size.

Whisk the egg white and brush over the top of the dough. Sprinkle the remaining seeds onto the top of the dough, alternating the different types on each section of the loaf.

Bake in the oven at 400°F for 30 minutes or until cooked through. The loaf should sound hollow when tapped on the base. Cool slightly and serve.

HERBED CHEESE LOAF

Serves 8

This loaf is best served straight from the oven to obtain the full flavor of the herbs and cheese.

INGREDIENTS

1 package active dry yeast

6 cups white bread flour

1 tsp salt

1 tsp fine granulated sugar

1 Tbsp polyunsaturated margarine

3 Tbsp chopped fresh parsley

¾ cup shredded low-fat cheese

1 egg white

Place the yeast, flour, salt, and sugar in a large mixing bowl. Rub in the margarine. Add the herbs and cheese and stir in 2 cups lukewarm water. Bring together to form a soft dough. Knead the dough on a lightly floured surface for 5 to 7 minutes until smooth.

Divide the mixture into three equal portions. Roll each into a 14-inch sausage shape. Place the dough pieces side by side and cross them over each other at the top, pressing together to seal. Continue

working down the length of the dough, crossing alternate strands to form a braid. Seal the end by pressing together and fold both ends under the braid.

Place the bread on a nonstick baking sheet, cover, and leave in a warm place for 1 hour or until doubled in size. Lightly beat the egg white and brush over the loaf. Bake in the oven at 400°F for 30 minutes or until cooked through. The loaf will sound hollow when tapped on the base. Serve.

◀ *Seed Bread*

WHOLE WHEAT SODA BREAD

Makes 12 slices

This yeast-free bread is based on an Irish recipe where it is traditionally served. Made with whole wheat flour for extra goodness, it is filling, and ideal served with soups.

INGREDIENTS

1½ cups all-purpose flour

1½ cups whole wheat flour

2 tsp baking soda

2 tsp cream of tartar

½ tsp salt

2 Tbsp polyunsaturated margarine

1½ cups skim milk

2 egg whites, beaten

Lightly grease and flour a baking sheet. Sift the flours, baking soda, cream of tartar, and salt into a bowl. Add the contents of the sifter to the bowl.

Rub in the margarine and gradually mix in the milk and beaten egg whites to form a dough. Shape the mixture into a round on a lightly floured surface. Score into four triangles with a knife and place on the prepared baking sheet. Bake in the oven at 425°F for 30 minutes or until cooked. Serve warm.

CONTINENTAL PLUM CAKE

Serves 6

This is a deliciously light sponge with a difference. For best results the eggs should be weighed and the sugar, butter, and flour should each be the same weight as the eggs.

INGREDIENTS

¾ cup superfine sugar

¾ cup butter, melted and cooled

½ tsp natural vanilla extract

3 eggs, separated

1½ cups self-rising flour, sifted

¾ lb firm, small plums, pitted and halved

Confectioners' sugar, for dredging

Preheat a 375°F oven. Line the base of a 7½ x 10-inch roasting pan with wax paper.

Beat the superfine sugar and melted butter until light and fluffy. Add the vanilla extract and beat in one egg yolk at a time. If it curdles, add a little flour.

Whisk the egg whites until stiff and gradually fold into the creamed mixture alternately with the flour. Spoon into the prepared pan, level the surface and arrange the plums over the top.

Bake for about 40 to 45 minutes until risen and golden and no mark is left when you press it lightly with your fingertips. Allow to cool slightly before removing from the pan and the wax paper if serving hot. Sprinkle with confectioners' sugar and serve either hot or cold.

APRICOT BARS

Makes 8

These are very filling, healthy fruit bars. A delicious apricot purée is sandwiched between a shortcake mixture.

INGREDIENTS

1¹⁄₃ cups dried apricots, chopped

4 Tbsp unsweetened orange juice

6 Tbsp polyunsaturated margarine, melted

4 Tbsp clear honey

¹⁄₂ cup semolina flour

1 cup plus 2 Tbsp all-purpose flour

Lightly grease a 7-inch square cake pan. Place the apricots in a pan with the orange juice and simmer for 5 minutes. Drain if the juice has not been absorbed by the fruit.

Heat the margarine and honey in a pan until melted. Add the semolina and flour and mix well. Press half of the semolina mixture into the base of the prepared pan. Spoon on the fruit mixture and top with the remaining semolina mix, covering the fruit completely.

Bake in the oven at 375°F for 35 minutes until risen and golden brown. Cool for 5 minutes in the pan, then cut into eight bars. Remove from the pan to a wire rack, leave to cool completely, and then serve.

LOW-FAT CHOCOLATE CAKE

Makes 12 slices

This chocolate cake is very rich and a small slice will satisfy any chocoholic for a while.

INGREDIENTS

¹⁄₄ cup polyunsaturated margarine

1¹⁄₄ cups granulated brown sugar

2 egg whites

1¹⁄₄ cups all-purpose flour

3 Tbsp unsweetened cocoa powder, sifted

¹⁄₄ tsp baking soda

¹⁄₄ tsp baking powder

1 cup skim milk

Confectioners' sugar and cocoa, for dusting

Grease and flour an 8-inch round cake pan. Cream the margarine and sugar in a bowl until light and fluffy. Add the egg whites and whisk into the mixture until thick.

Place the flour, cocoa, baking soda, and baking powder in a separate bowl. Add the milk gradually to the egg white mixture, alternating with the dry ingredients. Pour the mixture into the prepared pan.

Bake in the oven at 350°F for 1 hour or until cooked through. Let cool completely in the pan. Turn out and dust with the confectioners' sugar and cocoa. Serve immediately.

Apricot Bars ▶

CARROT AND PRUNE CAKE

Makes 12 slices

The carrot and prunes make this a gloriously moist cake.

Take extra care folding in the egg whites as a heavy hand will result in a heavy cake.

INGREDIENTS

8 oz carrots

15-oz can prunes in fruit juice

1¼ cups granulated brown sugar

2½ cups self-rising flour

Grated rind of 1 orange

3 Tbsp semolina flour

3 egg whites

For the icing

¾ cup soft cheese

1 Tbsp confectioners' sugar, sifted

Ground cinnamon and orange rind,
to decorate

Grease and base line an 8-inch deep cake pan. Shred the carrots and place in a bowl. Drain the prunes and discard the juice and pits. Blend the prunes in a food processor for 30 seconds and add to the carrot with the sugar. Add the flour, orange rind, reserving a little to decorate, and semolina to the mixture, stirring well. Whisk the egg whites until peaks form and fold into the mixture. Spoon into the prepared pan and level the surface.

Bake in the oven at 375°F for 45 minutes or until cooked through. Cool in the pan for 10 minutes, turn out, and cool completely on a wire rack.

Mix together the soft cheese and confectioners' sugar for the icing. Spread on top of the cake. Decorate and serve.

INDEX